Radislav
Gandapas

THE

KAMA

SUTRA

OF

PUBLIC

SPEAKING

Ten chapters on how to give
and receive maximum pleasure
from a public performance

ISBN 978-1-909122-79-6

Acorn Independent Press

CONTENTS

To my wife, Anna, who taught me how to
love and be loved

PREFACE

I first met Radislav Gandapas during one of my training workshops years ago in Odessa, Ukraine. I can still remember him vividly that day, taking centre stage with his sharp wit and his easy-going demeanour. Having quickly won over the crowd, Radislav delivered an entertaining and instructive presentation on public speaking, which kept the audience engaged and enthralled. I can recall the audience's members' expressions of total satisfaction at the end. His performance set me up well because I was next.

Radislav's *Kama Sutra of Public Speaking* contains the perfect toolkit to take your public speaking skills to the next level. This book is highly informative and details the mechanisms of seduction between the speaker and the audience, and it is written in a light and humorous style. Radislav comprehensively shares his tips and experiences that made him the person he is today. He clearly demonstrates that public speaking is an art, which can be learnt and even perfected by anyone who wants to do so. This is a very enjoyable and useful read.

Allan Pease

International author of 10 #1 bestsellers including *"Body Language"*.

FOREWORD

We all know that communication skills are an essential ingredient of success in almost every sphere in life – politics, academic study, business, and management. You can try to rely on your innate social skills, but this will only take you so far. To really master the sensuous art of speaking in public – and enjoying it – you need to learn some of the secrets, skills and methods I've laid out in this book. You'll hopefully also benefit from the sample of FAQs from my website that I've added at the end of each chapter to give you a bit more detail on becoming the public speaker you want to be.

One more thing: it's important to note that this book is not a serious scientific dissertation on human communication – rather, it's hopefully a friendly and even entertaining introduction to the techniques I've picked up over the years, which have enabled me to create a very pleasurable and lucrative career for myself in the world of public speaking. As the old saying goes, a pleasure shared is a pleasure doubled, so I really hope you will find this book engaging, lively and fun to read, and that it's truly useful to any budding public speakers out there.

Yours truly, Radislav Gandapas

PRELUDE

How I became a teacher of communication, and what drove me to write this book.

One of the perks of being a famous and successful business trainer and motivational expert is hearing newly-wowed trainees saying nice things about you. Once, during a training titled "How to be a successful public speaker", I overheard a participant say the following about me: "This guy is amazing – he has a God-given talent for this stuff; no wonder he's the best there is!" Now, before you throw away this book in disgust, convinced it's just another egomaniac guru blowing his own trumpet, let me tell you why that quote is relevant to this book's theme. It's relevant because of the complete contrast with what one of my best friends had said about me a few years earlier when he heard that I was working as a teacher of communication: "How can he be teaching people anything about that? He has the communication skills of a boiled potato!"

So who was right? The starry-eyed audience member or the close friend who'd known me all my life? Well, in a sense, they were both right. The fact is that you are not reading a book written by a mystically self-confident genius of interpersonal skills, born with the gift of the gab, able to schmooze, sweet-talk and inspire straight out of the womb. In fact, I spent most of my early life with constant, low-level social anxiety that would explode into full-on extreme fear and panic if I was asked to do any kind of public speaking. It was this aspect of my life that my friend was referring to when he so kindly pointed out my resemblance to a boiled spud. But it's also true that I managed to overcome this abject terror and become the leading trainer in motivational and public speaking in Russia and the former Soviet Union. So my fan in the audience was also partly right – I did become really, really good at speaking in public, it just wasn't a God-given talent. And, in a nutshell, that's what this book is about – my chance to pass on the beautiful and empowering knowledge that I have acquired. The knowledge that very few people are born as natural public speakers, but with the right mental approach and application, ANYONE can learn how to not only get through it, but to actively enjoy it – to give and receive maximum pleasure from your public speaking. After all, if the guy with the communication skills of a root vegetable can do it, what's stopping you?

So before we get into how you can turn yourself into a public speaking Don Juan, let me tell you a little more about how I ended up working as a public speaking guru and writing this book...

It actually all began in childhood. My first childhood memory is not that of my father coming home after a long business trip and holding his unshaven cheek next to my sleepy face. It's not of Grandma's pastry. And neither is it of a fishing trip with my grandfather. In fact, my first childhood memory is that of public speaking. That's right – my earliest childhood memory is one of intense anxiety, confusion and discomfort. Imagine yourself in my shoes: "Radislav dear, be a good boy and get up on that chair and recite the poem you and I learned yesterday to these nice ladies and gentlemen," says my mum. In Russia, there is a long tradition of kids memorising large chunks of poetry and then reciting it in front of their classmates. But today is New Year's, so my mum wants me to recite it to some friends who have come round for Russian salad and pickled herring. It's a typical scene. The guests are relaxed and ready to applaud, thanks to a few pre-dinner drinks. Mum and Dad are standing by proudly, waiting for my star turn. I am the only one suffering immensely. I am so scared, I instantly forget everything I learned the night before with such great pleasure. All four stumbling lines. As I stand there, mouth gaping like a landed fish, with that unbearable heat rising in my cheeks and tears springing to my eyes, I suddenly run out of the room and throw myself onto my bed, crying hopelessly – utterly bereft at my total failure and the inevitable disappointment and disgust my parents are going to feel... No presents, sweets or embraces can bring me back to life. It's over. I have disgraced myself.

My parents have no recollection of this ever happening. The guests from that night don't remember anything about it. But I remember everything with crystal clarity. I have carried this childhood memory through a lifetime. It rang a bell of embarrassment and confusion in my mind for a long time when I had to speak publicly. More than once, colourful blurs would rush in front of my eyes, my knees would shake and my voice would give out when I had to come on stage. Exams at school, contests, important events and amateur concerts turned into torture.

Yet despite the crippling fear, as I got older and did well at school, the ordeal of public speaking became a regular occurrence in my life – but never without the horrors, the trembling and the panic. I did my best to avoid it, but when I had to, I would somehow find a way to drag myself through the whole ordeal, and always swear to myself afterwards that I would never do it again.

In Russia, we say that only two things happen to us in life: the thing that we want the most and the thing that we fear the most. All the way through university, I was preparing myself for a career as a research scientist (a job that, of course, would keep me safely in a laboratory and away from any stages). However, in one of those strange twists of fate that come along sometimes, after I graduated, I somehow found myself working as a teacher of Russian language and literature. To this day I can't tell you how it happened, but the fact is that as a teacher, I had found the perfect training ground to begin the process of getting over my fear of public speaking. Anyone who's had any experience of teaching can confirm that there is no harder audience than children. Kids are very demanding. There is absolutely no pretence with them – if you are not holding their interest within two minutes, they won't sit there making politely appreciative but fake sounds. They will just turn away, or get up and start wandering around, or pulling the hair of the child in front. But if the teacher is a good public speaker, the children's eyes start to sparkle. And that look in those eyes is hard to forget. So slowly, I started to get over the worst excesses of my fear as I clocked up the classroom hours, and became better and better at engaging with my "audience". This was the first step forward for me – having the discipline of those weekly lessons for groups of up to 30 kids and teenagers helped me to see that simple repetition and practise could go a long way towards taking a lot of the panic out of the process of speaking in public. So now, intrigued by the idea that I might actually be able to get better at this, I decided to move to Moscow and set up as a business trainer. And yes, the first time I trained a group of adults was STILL terrifying – clammy palms, dry mouth, the lot. However, the difference was that now I knew that, with a little practise and application, I could get over it – and who knew – maybe even get to be really good at this.

Later, the nature of my work forced me to appear in public increasingly frequently. At press conferences and presentations, at exhibition openings and gala nights, during seminars and roundtables, on the radio and TV. Luckily, my job has also allowed me to see great public speakers from our country and abroad. I followed their speeches, took note of different tools and "perks", and tried to use what I saw. I started to get better and better, and eventually, I was even asked to help out with the public speaking that other people were doing. I instantly found that helping other people deal with public speaking was both useful and pleasurable for me – and when lots of people wanted my help, I tried to get them together in a group and work with all of them at once. This is how my training course, "How to be a successful public speaker", was born. I have delivered this course in many cities and countries, and the things I've learned along the way are now gathered in this book.

When I held this training session, I saw how much difference the ability to speak publicly could make when you are talking to decision-makers. I also realised the huge importance of fear, and the many ways in which it deprives us of the chance to make our lives better and more interesting. In fact, for a long time, I was obsessively focused on how one can get rid of fear. It never occurred to me that public speaking could actually be a fully enjoyable, pleasurable experience in its own right – so it was a genuine surprise to find out that this is indeed the case.

Over the years, I've realised that a large number of books on public speaking are written by people whom I would not even trust with making a toast at my friends' party. I have discovered that so many of the things that I've been taught myself have turned out to be worthless. But among these piles of rubbish, I sometimes found a few rough diamonds – tools and methods that make a good public speaker. My own development turned into the process of cleaning, cutting and polishing up these diamonds and, as a result, I ended up with quite a little collection of them, to share with other people at my training sessions. The point is that a natural-born genius of communication would not be able to do what I do; geniuses can very rarely explain where their genius comes from, and so struggle to teach others how to do what they do. But I know what it takes to develop these skills over time. And I *can* teach others, because I have learnt it the hard way myself.

This journey was no walk in the park. Sometimes, I told myself, "Stop it, enough. Can't you see that this is not your thing? Try doing something else!" But with the passing of time, I learned from my own experience and kept falling back in love with the craft again. This happened year after year. Whenever I talk about this, I often think of Valentin Dikul, a famous Soviet weightlifter who spent years trying to recover from a horrific injury that his doctors had assured him meant a lifetime of paralysis. Using his own experience, he created a system of exercises that allowed him to overcome paralysis and agonising spinal pain. This system is now being widely used and he has his own medical research centres that are hugely popular in Russia.

I am purposefully not saying anything about the financial success a skilful public speaker can achieve. Most of you are already pretty clear on that front. To me, another thing is more important, and that thing is pleasure. We do many things for pleasure in life. We pay for it. We make many sacrifices for it. Why not take pleasure out of public speaking? Any public speaking. At meetings and conferences, during wakes and weddings, concerts and press conferences, on TV and radio, on stage and from your seat, standing, sitting... the opportunities to find this pleasure are everywhere!

INTRODUCTION

Why this book is called "The Kama Sutra of Public Speaking".

So let's get the obvious question out of the way: why is this book called "The Kama Sutra of Public Speaking"? Well, the whole purpose of the original Kama Sutra was to show that sex could be about so much more than the simple function of reproduction – "getting the job done", as it were. Instead, this ancient Indian text promoted the idea that sex should be celebrated as a pleasure in itself, and that people should find as many different ways to enjoy it as they could. My purpose in this book is to bring my readers the same "enlightenment" about public speaking – to show that public speaking doesn't just have to be about the "function" – making a sale, getting a contract, etc. – but can also genuinely be enjoyed as a pleasurable art in itself. In essence, the following 10 chapters will show you how to give and receive maximum pleasure from the act of standing up and talking in front of a group of strangers.

This book is based on two key insights that I've had during my time as a public speaking expert:

1   The average or even "good" public speakers can learn techniques to hold the attention of their audience and get their message across,

even if, like most people, they are basically uncomfortable about speaking in public. But to be a great public speaker, it is necessary to transcend artificial techniques for hiding nerves and genuinely feel the pleasure of being up on that stage in full flow.

2 The relationship between a public speaker and his audience is very, very similar to the relationship between the seducer and the seduced – with the public speaker in the classically "male" role, and the audience in the "female" role. [1]

To a large extent then, success in public speaking is a matter of biology. An audience's reaction to a public speaker is instinctual, not logical. Most of our success with an audience depends on **how** we look and **how** we speak. **What** we are saying is much less important when it comes down to that all-important impression we want to create.

Now, doesn't that sound like a typical case of boy meets girl? Aren't those subconscious animal impulses much more important in attracting us to someone than any logical appreciation of the facts they know or the opinions they have? Of course they are.

One other point I should make here is that, as our Kama Sutra metaphor unfolds, I'm often going to be talking about the public speaker as "he" or "the man"

[1] I should probably make it clear that I am not in any way suggesting that the primary purpose of public speaking is to physically seduce individual members of the audience. That would be unethical, and extremely creepy. It's just that I think the metaphor of seduction is one that works really well in analysing what makes a successful public speaker, and as we all know by now, a good mental image sticks in your memory much better than a collection of dry facts – and what's more memorable than a great love affair?

and the audience as "she" or "the woman". Please don't think that this makes me yet another uncivilised Russian brute with stone-aged attitudes. I'm well aware that as many women are involved in public speaking as men; it's just that, for me, the "male" and "female" principle is one we all understand intuitively. In both kinds of relationships, there is a reaction of the passive with the active, the impact and the impression, the yin and the yang, the male and female. The audience has a "female" collective psychology, meaning that anything that would normally work in a relationship with a woman will work with your audience, and vice versa – anything that isn't normally permitted with regards to a woman, isn't permitted with your audience either. At this point, I should point out again that my description of the audience as "female" is a rhetorical device to aid the understanding of public speakers of either gender – the "femininity" of the audience in this sense is applicable even if it is an entirely male audience.

Just like other intimate relationships, the connection between a public speaker and their audience should be designed to give the utmost pleasure to **both** parties.

For those of you who have experienced the panic and anxiety that public speaking can cause, this may seem like an absolutely crazy idea, but I promise you that, as you go through the following chapters, you'll see that it **is** possible for you to enjoy this process as much as your audience do.

So when you think of your public speaking as an act of seduction that has one purpose – maximum pleasure for both participants – then everything starts to get easier and more successful. Start to think of the introduction to your presentation as a gentle caress, your greetings and ice-breakers as foreplay, before you move on to the main event – building up to the towering climax of your speech. And don't think you can leave immediately after it's all over either. A little time basking in the afterglow – thanking them for their attention, murmuring what a great time you've had – and they're yours forever.

The audience can be charmed. They can be seduced. You can make your audience fall in love with you as easily as you can fall in love with your audience. I have fallen in love many times. And many times, I have cheated with a different audience. Sometimes my audience cheats on me with other public speakers, and that's when I listen to that other speaker and take notes: what was he doing differently, what made him more attractive than I am? What can I do to make them come back to me again? And I found it. And it worked. And the audience came back to me. So I have a few things to tell you. Let's turn the page...

Chapter One

HELP! Making Performance Anxiety Work For You...

This chapter is devoted to getting to the root of performance anxiety and its origin; why we always feel nervous before making a public appearance, and how to make it work to your advantage. It will also explain why it's necessary to learn to speak in front of an audience at all.

It's every man's worst nightmare. Everything is perfect: the delicious meal you cooked for her has been eaten, to general delight. Half a bottle of wine has followed, and now there's just you, her, the candlelight and some Barry White drifting out of the stereo. She has that look in her eyes, the one you've been waiting for, so you gently lead her by the hand into the bedroom... and then... suddenly your mellow, loved-up mood evaporates. Thoughts start flying through your head about what's going to happen next, and before you know it you're over-thinking and worrying. The spontaneity is gone, and without wanting to get too graphic things down below are not behaving the way you want them too... So you grit your teeth and try harder – but it's too late.

You've been gripped by performance anxiety, and I'm afraid your lady is going to leave unsatisfied. Of course, we men never admit that these things happen, but they do, to **everyone**. So what is performance anxiety, and how can we actually make it work for us – at least in our public speaking?

The first thing to say about anxiety is that a certain amount of it is completely natural and healthy. What we want to avoid is the excessive anxiety that paralyses memory, speech and the speaker's ability to use gestures and facial expressions. Overcoming this fear alone would allow hundreds or even thousands of people to speak publicly with success and pleasure.

So what exactly causes anxiety? In essence, it is nothing more than a complex of biochemical reactions that lead to a release of adrenaline into the bloodstream. What does adrenaline do? It improves your reactions and blood flow (including the one to the cerebral cortex), making you blush and your eyes sparkle (by moisturising the eye mucosa). So, to a certain extent, we don't want to fight it at all! Sparkling eyes? Energy and quick reactions? Healthy, glowing cheeks? That all sounds like a pretty attractive package to me – exactly what a brilliant public speaker needs to make an unforgettable impression! This is the energy that gets to the audience and keeps people on the edge of their seats, making them jump with excitement. Adrenaline is our ally. However, the problem comes when *too much* adrenaline gets into the bloodstream. That's when energy and excitement tip over into anxiety and eventually panic. This happens because modern man fears public appearances more than anything, with the possible exception of death. This is why, unless you are prepared for it, in those brief moments on stage, your body produces almost as much adrenaline as if you were in deadly danger. Essentially, right before a public appearance, we experience the same level of stress we feel on the battlefield with bullets flying around, or when a train is moving towards us at full speed, or when we are balancing on the roof of a skyscraper. And the logical part of our brain can tell us as often we like that it's absurd to compare speaking in public to being in a firefight, but from our body's point of view, the stress reaction is the same. Here's my view on why that happens: Human beings are fundamentally social animals – everything about our emotions and nervous system has evolved to help us live in groups. What happens to a social animal when its group has rejected it? In most cases, it dies. It will either fail to find food on its own and starve, freeze, as it's now unable to warm itself up alone, or simply fall prey to predators, without the defence of its group. So millions of years of evolution have led to us having a highly-developed nervous system that is extraordinarily sensitive to our relationship with other people around us. And, for our subconscious nervous system, ostracism from the group is literally a matter of life and death. So you see, there's nothing absurd about the panic that public speaking can cause at all – it's actually a testament to our incredibly powerful and intricately-developed defence mechanisms. The question is: can we overcome this built-in defence mechanism and get past the fear to become great public speakers? The answer, of course, is a resounding yes. The secret is to lower the subjective significance of the upcoming public appearance and take away the primal, deadly fear. Let's talk about what can be done to make it happen.

As most Russians will attest, the quickest and simplest way to relax is a nice shot of vodka. However, with regular public appearances, this will lead to alcoholism, followed by memory loss, lowered motivation, apathy, getting fired, and generally, a pretty miserable outcome. Alcohol also leaves your system very quickly and, when it does, it often induces precisely the opposite effect to the original feelings: despondency, atonia (lack of normal muscular control) and anxiety. You should not take any kind of tranquilisers either! They impair your reflexes and dull your reactions. The tempo of your speech will slow down. You may be less anxious but the quality of your presentation will suffer. So let's make an agreement right here and now: booze and drugs are not the answer! Instead, here are a few exercises that will help reduce your anxiety in the moments before your performance begins:

1   Vigorously move your jaw back and forth about 20 times. The pneumogastric nerve gets stimulated, the signal is then transmitted to the nervous system, noradrenaline goes into your bloodstream, and your emotional state stabilises.

2   When you are sitting and waiting to be called out to go on stage, let your arms fall down and relax. Imagine that they have become ridiculously long, so long that they hit the floor... (The ladies may prefer to imagine that it's their legs getting longer, but that's a completely different story.) Now channel the tension you are feeling into the

ground. Feel it leave your body. But don't get too distracted because it's already the second time they've called out your name...

3   Work with your wrists, move your fingers, warm up your hands. You have already done this intuitively so many times. Doctors and psychologists say that warming up your hands not only helps lower the paralysing effect of anxiety but also stimulates your speech organs, and increases your aptness and eloquence. Science hasn't yet come up with a satisfactory explanation for this. Astrologers interpret it this way: Mercury rules hands in the human body as well as commercial abilities and speech. By warming up our hands, we activate Mercury and, in turn, our speech. To be honest, it really doesn't matter why – it works for me, and for most of the people I've trained, so give it a go.

4   Walk at a good pace; swing your arms – don't worry if anyone's watching! Any physical activity that gets your heart rate up relieves nervous tension.

5   Think about how your body behaves when you are afraid of something. Your chin drops towards your chest and you hunch your shoulders as if preparing for a kick to the head. Since the connection between our mind and body is a two-way street, you can influence your emotions by influencing your body. Lower your shoulders, lift your chin up, and straighten your spine. You should hold the posture of a calm and confident person, even if you don't feel like one.

6   Take slow, deep breaths. This is the way a calm person breathes. When we are anxious, our breathing is shallow and hurried. Our mental state determines how we breathe. And vice versa.

Slowly does it...

Right before the start of a presentation, get in the rhythm of speaking emphatically, slowly and calmly, even though you're not on stage yet. It's important to remember that time flows differently for you and your audience. When you are on stage, all the processes in your body happen faster, and rapid jerky speech can seem completely normal to you. The audience thinks that you are talking a mile a minute and perceives it as a sign of your uncertainty, and of the desire to get out of this nightmare as soon as you can. If you make a conscious effort to speak very slowly for an hour or so before your public appearance, you can avoid this problem.

The presence of people who are important to you – bosses, relatives, friends – in the audience is an additional factor that may enhance your anxiety. This is because, in our subconscious, there is an internal censor that we connect to the people who are important to us: in our childhood, it is often our father; when we grow up, it's our boss. We unconsciously believe that this person has the full and undivided right to judge, pardon and punish us. These are mind games. If there are people who are important to you in the audience and you feel that your anxiety is related to the fact that their opinion is important to you, remind yourself that you are there to help and instruct them and that they are not there to judge you.

Be goal-oriented

You have a goal and you will do everything you can to reach it. We are often too preoccupied with ourselves and the impression we make. If we are fully honest with ourselves on this, we'll remember plenty of situations in life when we could not achieve what we wanted because we were too afraid to look stupid, to be thought of as an idiot. Maybe you didn't invite a girl you liked to a dance, and your more confident friend swooped in instead. Maybe you couldn't bring yourself to push for a promotion and it was taken by a colleague. Maybe you didn't support a friend in an argument... didn't shine at the party like you wanted to... didn't dance at your friend's wedding... didn't go through with that bungee jump... didn't... didn't... didn't... It's time to end the list. Just concentrate on the job you are there to do – deliver maximum satisfaction with your public speaking, and don't let yourself get caught up in worrying about what they're all thinking about you. By the way, this insight is not just relevant to public speaking. Marmontel, a French philosopher, once said:

> *"He who checks his own behaviour against public opinion is not sure of himself."*

Remember these words.

Here are two exercises you can do that develop this idea:

The first one is called "Who is in the cage?" Before and during your public speaking event, imagine that it is not the audience who came to see you, as if they were in a zoo, but that it's you who is going to look at *them* and how they are behaving. Remind yourself of this image during your presentation. Observe the audience. Keep a mental note of funny moments, or interesting reactions.

The second exercise is called "Bunnies". For five minutes, close your eyes and imagine that you are not going to be talking to an auditorium full of human beings, but are in fact addressing an audience of rabbits. White, furry, pink-eyed and impossibly cute. Imagine the bunnies' ears in great detail, how you can see little veins in those ears. Imagine how sweet they are when they twitch their noses. Look at their frightened eyes... it's impossible to stay nervous in a room full of rabbits.

On the subject of imagining your audience a certain way, I imagine some of you are already thinking of the old chestnut of imagining them all naked. For my money, the people who spread this idea should have been banned from ever being allowed to give advice on anything, ever again! There are two reasons for this. If you've ever had a dream in which you stood naked in front of fully-clothed people, you must remember the feeling of discomfort. If we are speaking publicly and use this tool, we can subconsciously imagine the embarrassment our "naked" audience is feeling, and empathise with it, making us feel embarrassed right when we really don't want to.

And more obviously – imagining a room full of naked people tends to lead our minds to wander to thoughts of the bedroom... and although this whole book is based on the idea that public speaking can be *like* sex, it's probably a little too distracting to be thinking about *actual* sex during your presentation.

More on anxiety

Anxiety affects us bodily and mentally. In terms of the body, when we are anxious, we shiver, slouch and "shrink" into ourselves physically. The main mental effect is on our imagination, which shows us scary pictures of failure, public humiliation and the disgust of our peers. This feeling then gets imprinted on our memory – which tends to store the events with the strongest emotional content. This in turn means that, over time, we tend to store up a lot of memories of "failure" and "humiliation", leaving us even more blocked when it comes to just getting on with the job. In order to start putting our anxiety in its place then we have to fight back using the same weapons – the body, the imagination and the memory. We have already spoken about how to use your body and imagination. Now let's talk about memory and experience. Firstly, I am completely against the frequently recommended practice of analysing your performance and looking for mistakes. This is exactly what creates the distorted image of ourselves as weak orators, making constant mistakes in our minds. When you try to remember how you did, concentrate on the things that were successful – on the things that you managed to do well. Try to remember what impressed the audience the most. Remember that and use it again. You will never do everything perfectly. If you look hard enough, you can always find something that could have been better in any public speaking you do. Accept that, move on and focus on the things you **can** and **do** get right. A boxer, for instance, will never have a perfect bout without a single punch getting through his guard, or all of his own punches hitting the mark. He will never even be able to master all the types and combinations of punches equally well. But he will always have his own unique punches that are hard to resist. You too should have your own set of tools that almost always work. You will find them if you start focusing on the positive moments of your public appearance.

Lifestyle and worldview changes

These next tips often cause some resistance at my training sessions – mainly because they involve people making some fairly significant changes to their lifestyles. Of course, success in public speaking is possible without them – but you will find the whole thing much easier if you can take the following steps:

Get healthy: A professional public speaker must be in good physical shape – healthy blood vessels, a trained heart and lungs. This doesn't just allow you to put all your energy into performance, but also helps with keeping the fear at bay. It's a complex process that I won't go into now, but in my experience, everyone I know that has quit or cut down on drinking and smoking and begun doing regular exercise felt much more confident on stage and in life.

Get a love life: A professional public speaker should have a healthy sex life. We're talking quality, not quantity here – but you definitely shouldn't be repressing anything.

Get some perspective: One of the most valuable things you can develop as a public speaker (and as a person) is a sense of perspective. In moments of high stress, we all tend to ascribe far too much meaning and relevance to events – which in turn leads to us freezing with fear. I'm not saying that you should try to be blasé and cynical, and pretend that your public speaking event doesn't matter at all. Of course it matters, and you should prepare for it assiduously. But you need to find a balance, and I suggest that you cultivate the attitude that it is really just a game. A game you really, really want to win, for sure. But a game that you won't be absolutely devastated about if you lose. In fact, with a little practise, you might even realise that even if you do lose, there's still pleasure to be had. It is not normal if, after your speech, your internal voice rages on like this:

> *"What the hell was that? This is a complete failure! How am I going to look people in the eye?!! I am never going to do this again! I knew I was useless all along..."*

This is a sign of amateurishness. Imagine if the great Soviet pole-vaulter, Sergey Bubka, had thrown a tantrum every time he hit that crossbar.

You'll know you are heading in the direction of mastery and professionalism if your internal monologue is a bit more like this:

"Right. Today I didn't do that good a job. Why? My speech was too long. I didn't really pay attention when the audience started drifting off from the excess of statistics. I overdid it with technical jargon. I only maintained eye contact with one part of the audience. I barely moved on the stage. I rushed through the ending, it was confusing. Great! Let's work on it and see what happens. When is my next public appearance?"

This kind of accepting but determined mentality is summed up nicely by an old Russian joke: "Ushuyev, the plumber, decided to fight the urge to drink. The urge won today but the rematch is scheduled for tomorrow."

It is important to remember that even your worst speech is not the end of the world, or your life – professional or otherwise. The universe will not shrink to the size of a pea. The planets will not go off their course. The Mississippi River isn't going to suddenly change its course and flow to Texas... NOTHING REALLY BAD WILL HAPPEN!!!

If you understand and feel this deeply, the rest will be much easier.

And another thing. A public speaker has a finite amount of energy. Part of it is used to support his or her own body. Part of it goes to support brain activity. These are constants. The rest isn't much, and should be spent on getting the message to the public. If this energy is wasted on evaluating yourself, and internally criticising how you look and how it's going, it makes everything a seriously uphill battle.

Concentrate on the most important thing – on achieving the GOAL of your speech.

Maybe the following opinion shared by many experienced public speakers will help you: paralysing fear of public speaking is a normal thing for a beginner. With constant practice, the fear gradually goes away and is replaced by excitement and pleasure. The problem is that the fear will go away much later and you need to make a public appearance today. If you start running away from fear, it will follow you throughout your life. Go towards it and, sooner or later, you will see that you have left it behind. Take every public appearance as a personal challenge. Accept this challenge and achieve success.

"Easy for you to say!" you're probably thinking right now. And you are right. It is easy for me to say. Precisely because I practise what I preach.

Now let's try to figure out why one needs to learn how to be a good public speaker

The answer to this question seems obvious: to be more effective in influencing your audience's decisions, to have it lean towards the actions you want, to not fear any audiences and clearly state your thoughts, to help develop your business and to move up the career ladder; in the end, to reach your life goals faster and more effectively. All of this is true. But this is not all of it. We are missing what might be the most important thing. Life should bring pleasure. Or, rather, we have to go out and find pleasure in life. Today, when talking in front of other people, many of us feel discomfort. But we should try to get pleasure out of every single one of our public appearances! And it is possible. It is possible exactly because today, we feel fear. Almost everything that brings us pleasure today scared us in the past. Was it scary to go parachuting the first time? Of course! But when you did it, it was awesome. At first, it's scary to drive a car. But today, it's a pleasure hardly comparable to anything. Let's be honest, wasn't even sex something we were really scared of at first? But after a while, it's a genuine pleasure. And if we hadn't, we would have been deprived of such great pleasure. Let's learn to not just talk to the audience but to get pleasure out of it, because everything that a person does with pleasure is the right thing to do.

FAQ Chapter One

1

Dear Radislav, I'm a well-educated young presenter, but I can get intimidated when I have to perform in front of a largely middle-aged male audience with quite a high social status. Taking into account that the basic opinion of someone is formed in the first few seconds, what should I be doing to make a good impression? Thank you, Genia.

The first thing you need to do is avoid the rivalry in any kind of field and you should say this out loud. The audience you are describing often have a habit of competing. Sometimes, it is done in order to prove to themselves that they are worthy of the attention of others. Frequently, this is how they reach their high social status. But that's all psychology and it's not the point I'm making. The point I'm making is that trying to be cool in front of them is definitely not the way to go. Their only desire will be to put you in your proper place and that's something you want to avoid because it will not help to improve your performance. That's why you're going to need phrases like: "I'm not the one to teach you, but let me tell you something interesting...", "Of course you already know that, but here's a new twist..." Good luck!

2

Dear Radislav, I have a problem with transforming my thoughts into words. I need to talk in front of a large number of people and it's just so frustrating that putting my thoughts into coherent language takes such a long time. I always end up thinking that I look like a fool in front of people and that they are judging me and so on. This makes it even worse and I lose my confidence completely. Although I can usually come up with a quick retort to a question in my head, actually saying it out loud is always a problem. If you could tell me how I can get rid of this problem, I will be very grateful. Thank you, Misha.

As I mentioned before, the speaker and audience get into a sort of an "intimate relationship", where the performer gets the male role, regardless of his biological sex, and the audience gets the female role. If you start thinking about whether the audience loves you or not – that would be taking the female role and that doesn't work. A man doesn't think about the impression he gives; he thinks about his communicational goal, thus making the impression just a side effect. Although of course we all know men who are obsessed with their image, and those men would do anything for a woman's praise. Funnily enough, these types of men (in my personal experience) are highly unpopular amongst women. In reality, women are much more attracted to men who are professionally doing a good job without caring too much about their evening attire.

Does a man rescuing a child from a fire think about what he looks like and whether his jumps are dramatic enough? Does a female baseball player check her makeup before hitting the crucial home run? Does a scientist wonder how much he resembles Rodin's

"Thinker" when he comes up with a brilliant theory? At this moment, all of them are doing their job and they couldn't care less about the impression they might be giving to the public. As for the other people, they will respect them for what they accomplish, not for what they look like while doing it.

So your main objective here should be the idea you are trying to bring across, not the impression you give while doing it. Talk to yourself before the lecture. It's very important that you say your lecture all the way through (even if it's only in your head), especially the parts you want to present to the listeners and what result you are expecting of them. And during your speech, try asking yourself: "The thing I am saying now, does this bring me closer to my goal or take me further away from it?"

That's exactly why I don't recommend that my students go to public performance classes at a theatre school. Because the acting profession is all about image. An actor is completely absorbed in his looks, the impression he is giving, and how much the audience likes him and so on. He gets satisfaction when the audience claps their hands off. This impression-oriented profession influences most men in the sphere.

You have a mission and one simple parameter will tell you whether or not you have succeeded: have you reached your goal or not? That is it.

Your "problem" had nothing to do with complexes; you simply had the wrong set-up and starting point. It should get better from now on.

3

Dear Radislav, I have recently become a TV anchor. During rehearsals, I was very much at ease in front of the camera and everyone was expecting me to do well when the airtime came. And I did – my first live broadcast was spectacular, I was speaking freely with the TV audience, and the reviews were great. It wasn't until later that the problems began. After each live feed, as soon as I heard our sound engineer in my earpiece say, "Back to the studio", I would get stricken with horror, my neck would stiffen, and I could barely lift my head up to look at the teleprompter. The expression on my face caused a lot of our viewers to call the station and ask who was being mean to the anchor. The worst part was that I've now got fixated on this feeling and cannot get rid of it. Maybe I need to keep my back straight so that there is no strain on my spine or maybe it's all psychological? I don't know. Can this problem be fixed? (Please do not tell me to go to the masseuse...) Looking forward to hearing from you, Pavel.

This problem is both psychological and physical. The two go together hand in hand. I won't send you to a masseuse but it might be worth seeing a therapist. TV companies that care about the mental health of their hosts provide them with constant psychological support because working live on air demands a high level of stress resistance. That is why I devote a big part of my public speaking trainings to this very subject. For some reason, a lot of the time, people tend to believe that it is enough to just have the knowledge of how to speak to an audience.

Coming back to your problem. Try to remember how it began and what could have caused this feeling you are now experiencing. When was the first time you felt it? Try meditating or playing relaxing music to help yourself unwind and de-stress, and think back to that day. Imagine this situation in detail, experience the same feelings you went through on the day. Now consciously "rewind the tape" and play it again, but this time with a happy ending. If the cause was the sound engineer scolding you, instead, imagine him praising you; if it was the camera operator who was looking down on you, imagine him looking at you with admiration. This method works in other situations too and you may be able to work it out without seeking professional help. But given the nature of your job, if I were you, I would definitely pay a psychologist a visit. On the other hand, the reasons for this may lie outside of the realm of your work. I would need more information for a more detailed recommendation, but for now, try to process what I have written and maybe it will be enough to steer you in the right direction.

4

Dear Radislav, I find it very difficult to speak when I am standing in front of an audience. My mouth dries up, it's hard to control the sound of my voice, and I just feel very nervous. Even if I'm calm before going on stage, it still turns into a problem as soon as I get there. What should I do? Train my voice? Drink water? I'm lost. Please help. Anna.

Hi Anna. You know, some people would drink something much stronger than water to calm their nerves. You might think that knocking back 50ml of something strong is not that bad an idea, but there are drawbacks to look out for. See, at first, you feel at ease and confident; your panic goes away and you're quick on your feet with a joke or a retort, etc. This is of course no surprise, because whatever you drank widens blood vessels, activates the circumferential blood supply and throws a powerful stimulant into the bloodstream. But don't get too excited about this just yet, because the effect doesn't last long. Because you are up on stage, doing nothing but talking, the alcohol that you just drank evaporates and leaves your body through your mouth. Perhaps you heard that musicians like to get a good drink before a performance, and the only ones who don't drink are trumpet players and saxophonists. Because it would be a waste of good alcohol, as they are blowing air into a musical instrument for two hours in a row. The same thing happens to speakers, because they talk non-stop. And then comes the phase where the body goes into an opposite reaction – the blood vessels contract, proteins flood the bloodstream, the speaker's thoughts slow down and words begin to mix up. All in all, alcohol is not the best way to go in solving the problem of "stage fright".

It will be smarter if we try to understand why performing is a problem for you, even when you're not scared beforehand.

Throughout our life, we often find that our unconscious (the animal part) and our conscious (the rational part) get into confrontations. The unconscious is based on survival instincts and, as such, tries to care for our wellbeing as much as possible. It protects us from dangers, keeps us from problems, makes us cautious, and sometimes it goes overboard, making us plain lazy. The best thing for the unconscious would be if we resigned ourselves to a sofa in front of a TV, because that would present no threat to us whatsoever. When a person tries to achieve something: goes for a better job opportunity for instance or joins a gym, the unconscious instantly registers this as a potential menace and sends the person back to the sofa. The unconscious is oblivious to such pleasures as art, luxury, financial success; its only concern is survival at any cost. When there is a chance of success, it whispers, "What are you doing? Big money is a big risk! Something bad might happen to you!" or, "If you do this, they will think you're a fool!" It is the unconscious that makes us notice all the dangers that come with putting yourself out there and achieving your goals. Those who are able to overcome the spooks of the unconscious obtain success, while those who don't return to the sofa. Public speaking is a symbolic claim to be a leader. The unconscious despises it because being a leader means being responsible for reaching a goal. You become responsible for other people as well. This necessity to be active and fight in order to keep your leadership status makes the unconscious go into pure agony.

Did you know that 70% of illnesses have a psychosomatic nature? That means that we don't get sick because something is wrong with us, but because it's all in our heads and it is convenient to fall ill. Not for us, but for the unconscious. That way, there is no responsibility on us to fulfil expectations. It's very interesting, how the majority of people who love their job get sick less, and if they do, it's usually on the weekend, whereas those who don't like what they do fall sick during the week and get better closer to the weekend. It also often happens that as soon as a person realises that his unconscious is benefitting from his illness, he gets well.

What does this have to do with public appearances? Well, the unconscious tries to make them as difficult as possible for you, so that, on an instinctive level, you would not want to attempt it again. Even if you are not scared, your mouth still gets dry, your hands shake or sweat, you get a stomach-ache, your voice starts trembling, you start gasping for air and stuttering. All in all, it's hard to call this a pleasurable experience. The unconscious tries to drain all the ambitions out of you by screwing around with your body.

What to do then? Try to find a dialogue with the unconscious. Try to find a common language with it. How does the unconscious treat you? Not only does it try to convince you with physical pain that it's not a good idea, but it also has your imagination create horrible pictures of failure and catastrophe. So the unconscious links to the "experience", "body", "images" categories, and that is how you should "communicate" with it.

Let's start thinking about this from the end. Have your imagination create the most horrible, scariest and almost unreal outcome of your performance. You can take it to an absurd level. Imagine that people are throwing rotten tomatoes at you because of how awful your speech was, that some are even trying to hurt you, others are storming out of the room, maybe your best friend stands up in the middle of your speech and says:

"I can't believe how bad you are at this! I don't want to know you anymore!" In other words, imagine the most horrifying disaster that can happen during and after your speech. Once that's done, you need to remember to end this little exercise on a positive note, so tell yourself that none of these scenarios can or actually will ever come true. Now, imagine your speech going the way you want it to go, with people listening attentively to you talk, imagine applause at the end, their smiles and congratulations.

Secondly, try to work with your body. Move actively, jump around and wave your hands. This will help you release the adrenalin that you have. Now, lower your shoulders, straighten your back, and raise your head – that is what a calm and confident person looks like. Take 20 slow, deep breaths – this is how a calm person breathes.

And finally, practise speaking in front of people on a regular basis; take every opportunity that comes your way. Don't concentrate on the things that didn't go well; memorise the things that did. Play them over and over in your mind, returning to the experience of success. What you're doing here is creating a positive set-up for your future speeches. And it will not be long before the stuttering will go away, your mouth will stop drying up and your body will move smoothly across the stage.

CHAPTER TWO

The Algorithm for Success

This chapter sets out a little algorithm for preparing your public speeches. It also covers the importance of clearly identifying your goal in simple language, and the tools you can use to achieve this.

How do you make a successful public appearance? And what do we even mean by success? Ecstatic applause? A flow of interested questions from the audience? Or is it something else?

This depends on the goal you have. If your goal was to get a little applause and you heard it, is this a glorious success? Nope! It just means that you set a too-easily-achievable goal.

The goal of any activity, as you very well know, lies outside of the activity itself. Applause is just something that comes as part of the package. What is your real goal? "Make an impression! Get the message across! Make people remember you! Make them like you!" say the participants in my training sessions. "But why?" I ask them, "For what purpose?" And this is when they usually have a eureka moment! To make this process faster, let's ask the main question: "What should your audience DO after your speech?"

Vote for your party
Buy your product
Accept your bid for an ad campaign
Give you a raise
Sign a contract with your company

Be completely honest with yourself when you answer this question. Write the answer down. Think about what reaching this goal will give you. The recognition of the goal behind your speech will not only help you to better prepare the text of the speech but will also give you the necessary strength and inspiration before and during your presentation. If you never lose sight of the fact that your public speaking has a real-world, practical objective beyond the speech itself, then you will always find the energy to achieve it. No goal – no enthusiasm, no energy, no presentation.

Once we have identified the goal that will truly motivate our speech, we can turn to the actual preparation. Now, I know algorithms aren't particularly sexy (for most people anyway) and this is supposed to be a Kama Sutra of public speaking, but I find that this little algorithm or system works every time I need to plan a presentation:

In line with the wonderful modern world of the internet, I call it the WWW system:

Who – **W**hat – Ho**W**

The idea of this simple template or algorithm is to get you over the "writer's block" phase of preparing your presentation. Speeches are often difficult to write because, although we may have a head full of thrilling metaphors and witty one-liners, we don't have a structure to put them into. This template allows you to build that structure straight away, meaning you can avoid those endless hours of procrastination, and trying to find "inspiration" while you stare at a blank page. After all, no doctor will start treating a patient without asking him questions about his wellbeing; no military commander will begin the attack without finding out the exact positioning of his enemy's troops; so the first thing we need to do is ask ourselves a couple of questions. So here goes:

Who?

Who are the people in your audience, what kind of people are they? Where do they work? What motivated them to come and hear you speak? What are they expecting? What are they hoping to hear? What are they going to do with the information you give them? What are their fears? What are their joys? What do they already think of you and, for example, the company you represent?

At this point, you may be objecting that the people in the audience are all individuals and that it is impossible to get a useful sense of who they really are. This is only true up to a point. If all of these people got together in one room, at the same time, and on the same occasion, there must be things that unite them. Try to find those things.

What?

The next thing you have to consider is WHAT YOU WANT THEM TO DO AFTER YOUR SPEECH.

Remember, it is so easy to get lost in the fear and excitement of speaking publicly, and to lose sight of the fact that every moment on that stage serves a purpose. Always keep in mind WHAT you want the speech to achieve in the minds of your audience, and you can't go too far wrong.

HoW?

So, we've identified *who* we are speaking to and *what we want them to do* after our speech; the final, critical question is "how"? How are we going to achieve the result we want? Which arguments, rhetorical tools and metaphors are we going to use? Which facts might bore them? Which clichés will have them rolling their eyes?

I use this system myself when I prepare both speeches and training sessions. When I am asked to help prepare a speech for an event as a consultant, the first questions I ask the person who invited me are all based on the Who-What-HoW system.

Case Study:

Not long ago, I had the pleasure of doing some consultation work with two executives from a big Russian company on a presentation they were preparing for a new product pitch. This job turned out to be one of the greatest successes for Who-What-HoW yet. The main difficulty they faced was that the product had to be presented to two different audiences, one day apart: the first being chief executives of (Moscow) ad agencies and the second, regional broadcasting representatives. The text of the speech was ready, but while rehearsing, something felt wrong – and the practice audiences just weren't buying it. After spending 10 minutes with my clients and getting down on paper the answers to the questions in my template, everything became crystal-clear: the result the executives wanted from each audience turned out to be completely different. The projected audiences themselves were totally different too – they had different motivations, concerns and expectations. We quickly worked out two alternative approaches to the same presentation, based on my algorithm. In the end, both presentations were really successful, and the company is now reaping the benefit.

Once you have the outline...

What do you do next? We have come up with a portrait of our audience, decided what to expect from them, and chosen the arguments and tools to persuade them to perform certain actions. Time to prepare the text. How do we get ready for a speech? Write... write... write... Wrong. Even in the cerebral cortex, different areas are responsible for writing and speaking. When a speaker prepares for a speech in writing, you can hear it. His words sound unnatural, even if he has memorised the text and speaks without looking at the notes. Even if you've read the notes a thousand times and committed them to memory, you are kidding yourself if you think that the audience can't tell the difference between a prepared speech and natural communication. And, in most cases, the likelihood of them trusting what you're saying when they can see that you are reading from a script can drop to almost nothing. It is very hard to get what you want that way, so I suggest you approach it differently:

Do not write your text.

Do not even bother writing an outline. Not even the ideas.

Start practising your speech by just saying it out loud. Impromptu. Don't stop. Don't correct yourself. Don't start over. Say the whole speech from the beginning to the end the way you see it now. When you are done, say it one more time. And I mean, say it! Don't just say it in your head, but out loud. Do it a few more times. It doesn't have to be loud, you can be quiet, but you have to say it. Do it a few more times. Play around with it. Add bits in, take bits out. It's OK if you forget an excellent line in your sixth attempt that felt so right in the third attempt. Don't worry about having anything set in stone just yet. Rehearse it over and over again. As you are building towards the final version, start thinking a little more carefully about body language and gestures. Slowly start timing yourself and altering the speech to meet the time limit. A really useful suggestion is that you walk in a quiet place when you are getting ready for a public appearance, ideally somewhere near a river or a sea. The organisers of my training sessions in different cities know that one of the first questions I ask is "Is there a body of water anywhere near here?" In a few days, when you notice that you have been repeating the speech almost word for word, over and over again, *then* note down the main ideas. But no more than seven. Your speech is almost ready. You can start preparing the visuals and answers to the possible questions. I'll talk about this in more detail in chapters six and eight.

FAQ Chapter Two

1

Dear Radislav, I sometimes have to take part in long conferences that usually take place around a big table where everyone present has a different status in the company and speaks out of turn without any particular order. How do I join in the conversation without raising my voice or cutting across someone mid-sentence? Thank you so much, Joseph.

In this sort of set-up, it is best to insist from the start that everyone follows one order of communicating. Ideally, there would be a chair (chosen or appointed) that will host the discussion and manage it in an orderly fashion. You can volunteer to be that chair. In this case, you will have to be very strict about keeping to the rules. If it's a brainstorm type of meeting then one set of rules apply; if it's not then a different set, but the host needs to manage both tempo and order accordingly. You need to state from the beginning what the subject that everyone is talking about is, and what result/conclusion/decision you are planning to achieve at the end of it.

2

Dear Radislav, I once read that you said the following: "When you are speaking in front of an audience, you should look as if you couldn't care less about the result of your speech." What technique would you recommend that will help me act more carefree in front of the audience? Best wishes, Maria.

The best tool I know of is *actually* feeling that you do not care about the outcome of your speech. Although this does not rule out the drive to achieve your goal. You should clearly see (in as much detail as possible) all of the possible results of your speech. From the most unsatisfactory one to the most magical, and internally accept all of them. It might sound unusual, but this is one of the secrets of public speaking. No matter what happens, you should not worry. Not even one bit. No mad joy or inconsolable grief should get to you. Nothing!!! Although, I understand that it's much easier said than done.

3

Dear Radislav, my speeches look perfect on paper, but I have an extremely hard time saying them out loud. Even if I am perfectly familiar with the subject, it only takes one glance at my notes and then I can't look away after that. How do I break this vicious circle? Thank you, Polina.

Polina, I would strongly advise against preparing for your speeches in writing. My suggestion would be to draw pictograms, which would symbolise the outline of your speech. From now on, you are no longer to prepare for your speeches in writing. You see, by writing things down, you block the opportunity for your brain to come up with a unique turn of phrase because, ultimately, written communication and oral communication are two different things. I will not go into all the details on this subject; I would just hope that you take my years of research into this as a given and trust me. At first, it will be a little unusual and scary, because you'll feel as if your written notes are like a harness that's keeping you from falling, when, in fact, it's preventing you from flying. It will come with practice – you shouldn't be worried.

4

Dear Radislav, I need your professional advice with something. I perform lectures before an audience that is older than me, sometimes significantly. My lectures are often very long, sometimes for more than six hours. How should I conduct my performance so that the audience stays interested and pays attention throughout the whole of the lecture? Hoping to hear from you soon, Yana.

Dear Yana, is the audience so much older than you that special techniques are needed to keep them from falling into a long, lethargic sleep?! If this is the case, then remember that elderly, tired, unmotivated, nervous people and children have a much shorter attention span than the average middle-aged person. (I just imagined what would happen if you had to do a lecture for a group of elderly, tired, unmotivated, nervous people who had fallen back into childhood...)

What does this tell you? This tells you that you need to use more active ways of attracting and keeping the attention of the audience. Firstly, if the speech is to last half a day, I suggest, for humanitarian reasons, that you break it up with 15-minute intervals. One or two of those would be enough and you can announce them when you feel the audience is itching for a break. Of course, before the announcement of the break, there has to be some kind of emotional rise. At this moment, you can give your audience a compliment, sum up the things that you have said during the last part, announce what is coming up after the break, or make a funny joke.

Every 15-20 minutes, change the way you conduct the lecture. If you have spoken for 15 minutes straight, suggest it's time for questions, or show videos or slides, or walk to a completely different part of the room. For example, stand on the other side or even behind the audience for a bit. If you were speaking standing up, sit at a table, take off your jacket – if the format of the lecture allows it, of course. After a few minutes, stand up and put your jacket back on. You will see how the people sitting in the room will also straighten their backs. By the way, it is truly an amazing and inspiring thing for a speaker to see the people sitting in the room start to unconsciously repeat your moves, like shaking their heads, sitting back, smiling, opening their eyes wider, etc. That means you're fully connected with them.

Furthermore, actively involve the audience – that is a method that I suggest everyone should use. Ask the audience questions. Especially if you feel that it's time to shake things up. The questions can be quite simple: "Is everything clear?" or "Can we go on?" or "Are there any questions?" Bring someone out on the stage and ask him/her questions. This always brings life to a performance. Or approach someone with a question. You may use your female advantage and ask someone to hang a poster, move something, or turn off the lights, etc.

Use contrasting methods. Suddenly change the tempo of speaking from very slow to very fast and then back to slow. Talk quietly, then loudly. Stay silent for a minute. If you have had to stay in one place for a long time, walk actively around the stage for several minutes. Only don't make it look as if you were a caged tiger.

And of course keep eye contact with all of those sitting in the room. Pay special attention to those sitting at the sides and in the back. If there is a possibility of meeting your eye, then no one will dare to doze off.

I wish for your audience to have genuine interest in all your presentations, whatever age they may be.

CHAPTER THREE

Structure and the
Law of Composition

This chapter focuses on the structure of a speech: what it begins with and how it ends, where you should put the most important idea, and how to get your audience ready to receive this idea.

We all used to write essays at school; many of us took music lessons and some of us may even have written short stories. And what do all of these activities have in common? They are all based on a certain structure that I like to call the Law of Composition. Let's refresh our memories on how that structure looks:

1. Introduction – approximately 20% of the total work
2. Development of the theme – 60%
   - And let's not forget the "end" of this central section, which we can call the Culmination or Climax.
3. Conclusion – 20%

Once we start thinking about it, we can find different metaphorical versions of this Law of Composition in all sorts of different human activities and events. In music, we have the overture, the main movement, the crescendo, and the resolution. In cuisine, a good meal starts with an aperitif or a starter, goes through the main dishes, climaxes with dessert, and then gets rounded off with coffee and chocolates, depending on your tastes. There is clearly something about this pattern or structure that just feels... right. My own point of view is that this "rightness" comes from the very roots of our biological nature. (A good rule of thumb I use when judging metaphors or patterns of thought is: does this idea reflect what exists in nature? In this case, of course, I mean human nature.) If an idea seems to fit into what we know about how nature works, then I'll give it some serious consideration. If it doesn't, I don't. So when I look at that most primal aspect of human nature – the act of reproduction, I see a great example of the Law of Composition. (If some readers don't feel comfortable reading about sex, now would be a good time to skip to the next chapter...)

The fact is that people make love in accordance with the Law of Composition. Let's take a look at how the Law of Composition works for men and women's "intimate time". So, where a composer has his overture, our lovers have foreplay. This stage can go on for a while until they reach the point where there's no more holding back, and they become... ahem... "joined" and move on to the *main event*. (I hope I don't need to explain to adults how this bit happens.) At the end of the main part, if our lovers are lucky, there's the *climax* – which is short, intense and full of powerful emotions.

We can lose ourselves completely at this point, with no awareness of our surroundings. Out of this inertia stage, we slide effortlessly into cuddling and terms of endearment, coupled with murmurings of satisfaction at the deep, sensual joy we've just experienced. This would be our *conclusion*.

If you're not convinced yet, here's a few more examples of the Law of Composition. Let's start with illness or fever: first, you feel slightly under the weather, as the viruses begin to do their disruptive work in your body, even though you are still basically healthy; then you develop a headache. This is the *introduction*. The next morning, your headache becomes severe, your whole body starts to ache, and you begin to run a fever. The only positive thing is that you can take a sick day off work. That is the *main part*. The next day you experience an alarming night when your fever is so high your temperature is off the chart, your head spins as if you were strapped to the wheel of fortune, sweat comes pouring down like Niagara Falls, your relatives run around with mugs of tea and blankets... After hours of tossing and turning, you finally fall asleep at the crack of dawn. You later wake up to realise you feel much better. That was the crisis – the *culmination* of your illness. Even a young and inexperienced doctor can tell you that *the crisis* is a defining moment in any illness – there are only two options at this point – you will either pass over to the other side or get well. Either way, the temperature drops. It's a bit morbid to imagine the first scenario, so let's stick to the one where you get better. All in all, the fever is gone, you've regained your appetite, you are still a little groggy and have a minor headache but your doctor clears you to go back to work. This is the final part, or the *conclusion*.

Or how about a sporting example? Freestyle wrestling, for example, also includes our familiar four phases: headlock, tackle (pushing or tricking your opponent into a falling down throw, and pin down (the ultimate humiliation for your opponent). The Law of Composition is clearly at work again: the headlock is the *introduction*, tackle (when both wrestlers expend most of their energy to gain control of the move) is the development of the theme, the throw is the culmination, and pinning down to score the point is the *conclusion*.

The examples of this pattern in our everyday lives are endless, even if we never notice them. That's why, ultimately, I think of it as a naturally-occurring phenomenon, not just a man-made idea. That's also why I think anything that is done in line with this law will be much more successful than activities that ignore it. A public speaking event then, being a biological act like any other carried out by humans, has to follow the Law of Composition if you want it to be successful. If it does, then the audience will have an easier time of understanding the speaker, who will accomplish the original goal of their presentation with ease. If this law is not taken into account, despite all the brilliant arguments that the speaker might have, they will not be successful at their presentation and will then waste countless hours trying in vain to find the reason why.

That is why it should come as no surprise that, in my training sessions as well as in the video courses, I urge my students to use the *Law of Composition* when creating an outline for any public speaking event.

So let's take a look at what should be said at each stage of your presentation. I want to start by looking at the *introduction* and the *conclusion* together first, but before I explain why, let's bear in mind that, as important as they are, sexy foreplay and the tender caresses of the afterglow are not the same thing as intercourse. Likewise, appetizers and dessert, while tasty, can't really be described as a meal – just as the mild symptoms at the very beginning and end of a cold are not really the same thing as an "illness". The point here is that, even though neither of these stages actually contain the meaningful content of your presentation/ speech, they do serve important purposes: to establish emotional contact with the audience and to give them a genuine sense of an ending, so they can go home satisfied. The importance of these stages is something we need to keep in mind and not underestimate. A prelude before sex prepares the minds and bodies of two people for more intense sensations while caresses at the end of intimacy not only add but reinforce the sensations that have just taken place, leaving people with the desire to go and return to the same partner. A truly skilful lover really makes thier impression at these moments.

It is no secret that any type of communication happens simultaneously on two levels: the personal/ emotional level and the pragmatic/logical level (these two types of communication are often referred to as "left-brain" and "right-brain", with the left being rational and logical, and the right, emotional and empathic. I'm not sure it's true, but it is a useful metaphor). A public appearance is no exception, although there is a regular shift of focus between these two "modes" of communication during a speech. It is the main part of your presentation that mostly engages the intellectual element of your audience, while in the *introduction* and *conclusion* on the other hand interpersonal emotion is much more important. It is this emotional link that is fostered by the introduction and then reinforced by the conclusion that enables you to make sure your intellectual message in the main part is driven home and accepted by your audience.

An important point to bear in mind is that the conclusion is your last point of contact with the audience, so if you want your message to stay with them for any length of time after the presentation, you need to leave them with a skilful exit – maybe a final flourish or two. Not only will this leave them much more likely to help you achieve the goal of your presentation, it will also make them much more likely to come and see you speak in public again.

Always remember (and I know I've mentioned this more than once, but it is a very central idea) that the speaker creates an intimate connection with the audience, in which the speaker is a "man" and the audience is a "woman". There is a well-known stereotype that, in sexual relationships, the man needs much less time to get excited, and is much quicker to lose interest after the deed is done, than the woman. (Like all stereotypes, it's not completely true – but is used commonly enough for our purposes.) As a result, men are generally less interested in foreplay, and kissing and cuddling after sex. Even if they want to be more "into" it, their bodies don't really let them. Women are a different story altogether. A skilful and prolonged prelude may have a drastic effect on what a woman feels towards a man who has revealed himself to be a kind and compassionate lover, before the "main event" has even really got started. Likewise, the audience listening to you speak will make decisions and form opinions about you as a speaker, long before you get down to the main facts or arguments of your presentation. This is based on the empathy they feel towards you or the favourable psychological climate that can be created by you in the first few minutes of your speech and returned to at the end of it. This may seem like I'm rudely dismissing the actual content of what you have to say. That really isn't my intention, and of course, you can't cover up a complete absence of something to say with a nice introduction – but the fact remains that the process of making a decision about someone is mostly irrational and non-verbal, so the more you can do to create an emotional link with your audience from the beginning, the better.

An unskilled speaker, appearing before an audience, will behave more or less like an inexperienced lover in bed – they will unconsciously skip the introduction, quickly moving to the main part and, once that's over and done with, rush through to the culmination, and finally, dash off the stage. But now that we have covered what *not* to do, starting from today, you, as a speaker, will behave differently. May I remind you though that ideally, the *introduction* and *conclusion* should each take up no more than 20% of the whole speech.

Getting straight to the content of your presentation without a proper introduction to ease your audience in makes you the public speaking equivalent of the guy on holiday who drunkenly walks up to the beautiful woman at the poolside bar and says something along the lines of: "Hey sexy, you've got nice eyes. How about you and me head to my room to get to know each other better?" Other than in the wildest dreams of pubescent teenage boys, this never, ever works, and most of the time, will be greeted with a slap in the face or a thrown drink. And your audience's response won't be any different. You need to take time in courting and seducing them too. It's the only way to get the result you want. There is, of course, no need to take anybody out to dinner and a movie. A few minutes of *introduction* where you create the right emotional ambience, without giving away important information from the main body of your presentation, will suffice. So treat it accordingly and remember the "prelude to intimacy" metaphor. Since the audience is the "woman" in this relationship, she needs it more. The speaker can make do without the *introduction*, but the audience needs a prelude. And it's the skilfulness of this prelude that will eventually drive your audience "wild with passion". Start out with a gentle caress in verbal form, something along the lines of, "I've been looking forward to this presentation ever since I heard it was going to be for such a well-respected company as..." and then let it build up from there.

But before you start doing and saying anything, remember this – what do you do to seduce a beauty? Right, you look her in the eye. And, in your eyes, she sees a storm of emotion, she hears the murmur of the sea, the crying of seagulls, the shining of a hundred moons; so take a pause before you start talking and make eye contact with your audience. Let them get the impression that you are overflowing with desire to begin but your emotions overwhelm you. It is those first few minutes that, without a doubt, determine the success of a speech. The same way they determine the success of a love affair. If, for instance, you revealed yourself as a pushover and a cheapskate, it is very unlikely that you will be able to change a woman's mind on your third date, and vice versa: heroism and courtesy you show in the beginning will help you live happily together for many years.

10 options for the *Introduction*. Note that one presentation could combine a few of these simultaneously.

1. **An interesting fact** that is directly connected to the topic. Simple facts introduced with: "Did you know that..." or "Have you ever considered that..." seem to do the trick perfectly.

2. **An impressive figure or statistic.** This is a great way to introduce your speech, although I should warn you against simply stating the figure baldly. Even the most fascinating numbers alone aren't going to excite anyone. Use comparisons and imagery. A good example here would be of a speech the head of client services of a cell phone operator once gave. He started his presentation with the following introduction: "The average seating capacity of a football stadium is 100,000 people (the image of a stadium appears on the screen). Today, our company services 10 million subscribers. This is 100 football stadiums (the screen displays a table of 100 squares, each containing a zoomed-out image of the stadium)."

The audience reaction was surprised and interested, and the speaker had them hooked. All of this was achieved by taking the impressive but, in itself, meaningless number of 10 million and surrounding it with vivid imagery.

3. **Rhetorical Questions.** Don't expect your audience to ask questions and engage in dialogue with you at the beginning of your speech. You need to develop their interest in a discussion with you gradually throughout your time on stage, so at the beginning, stick to rhetorical questions.

4. **Tell a story.** This is something I'd like to call the "When I was on my way over here..." trick. An introduction with a story from the speaker describing something interesting he witnessed or overheard on the way to his presentation is usually engaging and interesting for an audience – even if they're not entirely convinced it's true. Of course, the speaker then has to find some way to connect this "random" event to the topic of their actual presentation and, in making this link, it is important to remember two rules: first, don't give away the correlation between what happened and the presentation topic straight away. Leave some space for intrigue. Second, whatever situation you're describing should have happened as recently as possible, meaning something that happened to you five years ago in Tokyo is much less interesting to the audience than what happened to you on the subway an hour ago.

5. **Jokes.** If you have been blessed with the rare gift of telling jokes or anecdotes that make people laugh, open with one that could be connected to

the topic of your speech, again, remembering not to give away the joke-topic connection too quickly. You might even want to come back to the joke at the very end of your speech and reveal the metaphor then. However, if you have not been blessed with this gift, I beg you to begin with *any* of the other options listed here. There are few more tragic sights than someone *trying* to be funny and failing.

6. **Feelings.** It has already been established that, to be successful on stage, you need to create an emotional ambiance. Personally, I don't know a better way of doing this than speaking about your own feelings. Being honest and sincere is a sure way to make people empathise with you. If you are a rather experienced public speaker, you can discuss a current event that has recently shaken the world/ country/town and what you feel about it. Be careful about expressing extreme fear or panic though – regardless of how great your overall speech is, showing anxiety to your audience will undermine your on-stage persona and their confidence in you. And also, remember that the feelings you are displaying should be consistent with the topic of your speech.

7. **Self-introduction** is always a good idea, even if most people in the audience know you already. Explain how the topic of the speech relates to you and why it's you who is on stage today and not anybody else. Mention your expertise in the given subject and talk a little about your accomplishments in the past.

8. **Outlining your speech** is the easiest and most "standard" of all the 10 options. All you have to

do is give a brief outline of the main topic, how long the speech is going to be, and what idea you plan to put forward – set the "rules of the game", so to speak. Something along the lines of this: "I have 20 minutes to tell you what our company accomplished in the last year. I will show you some figures and announce a couple of the changes that we intend to implement. Should you have any questions, please write them down and ask me after the presentation."

9. **Pay a compliment.** The introduction is the perfect moment to pay your audience a compliment. Everyone knows that an overly-exaggerated compliment sounds like sarcasm, so be subtle. Ideally, it should be brief, sincere, unambiguous, and reflect reality with a minor hint of embellishment. This can be done in four ways:

- Superlatives: ("You have the most incredible X here in...")
- Comparison: ("You have much better X here than those guys in ...")
- Intonation
- Combination of all three

What characteristics of the audience should you compliment? Anything from their appearance, age and maturity to their professional level, punctuality, or lack of the same. Example:

"They say that all geniuses lacked punctuality. That means the room is filled with geniuses, which makes my task as a speaker more

complicated, but at the same time, increases the pleasure from talking to you."

I often have people say to me that their audience is so diverse that there is no *one* thing that can be used to compliment all of them. I reply by saying that if a group of people got together at the same time and at the same place, there must be something that unites them; all you have to do is find what it is. And when you do, use *that* as the basis for a compliment.

10. **Common ground.** Another way to describe this option is "Friend or Foe", as it is based on the evolutionary fact that our brains all have a natural tendency to immediately pigeonhole new people we meet as either "Belonging" – (being like me, and therefore, a friend), or "Not Belonging" – (not like me, and therefore, a foe.) You can use this phenomenon to focus the audience's attention on what *you* have in common with them: common interests, age, occupation, interests, etc. This is a very important tool, especially as most psychologists point out that in the first few minutes of meeting a new person, we unconsciously try to analyse him or her and figure out if this person is dangerous. This is obviously not quite so important in the modern world – but the truth is that we haven't yet evolved past this tendency, which is why it's worth considering this approach. Naturally, we consider someone who we know or someone who at least looks similar to us as "a friend", so the first thing to do is to convince the audience that you are of no danger to them and to calm them down. Otherwise, they may not listen

to your arguments. This drive for the comfort of similarity and recognition is so powerful that the evidence for it can be seen throughout all human groups, from tribes to massive civilizations. The army wear uniforms, Indians use war paint, punks and hippies have Doc Martins, bell bottoms and Mohicans.

A few words about the *Conclusion*

OK, that's the foreplay out of the way – let's skip the main event for now and look at the conclusion of your speech. Obviously, mumbling "Thanks – that's it" and wandering off stage isn't going to cut the mustard – such an anti-climax could undermine everything you've achieved during the presentation itself.

The conclusion has to prompt an emotional outburst and it should make your audience want to applaud, so it needs to be directly correlated with the main idea of your speech.

The great news is that you don't need any extra magic to do this – you can either recycle or mirror the options for introducing your presentation! So, state your key points while paying attention to the main idea, talk about your personal involvement in the subject, remind everyone of the time limit, and pay a compliment to the audience's attention/thoughtfulness/awareness/ punctuality/sense of humour, recap what unites you all and make a joke if the situation calls for it. The most brilliant way to end would be to loop around to the first phrase/joke/point of your speech, creating a complete, connected ring of thought. In this case, an ovation is almost guaranteed.

What is *Culmination*?

In a work of music, culmination is a moment when the main theme has been developed to the maximum, and all the instruments are playing at once. In a work of literature, it is when emotions and conflict are at their peak, and we all know when it happens in sex. In a public speech, the *culmination* is the proposal or the idea, which you are presenting to the audience. Just like in music, literature and, sadly, sex, the culmination is a short-lived phenomenon, and that is the way it must be in your speech. It should be coherent, clear and brief. Don't make your audience try to guess; remember that the intellectual level of the audience as a whole is lower than that of each individual member. As we saw in the first chapters of this book, the *culmination* is the heart of your speech, and this is where you embed your call to action, so keep it short and clear. Much like in a relationship between a man and a woman, the many days of romancing and dating are great, but it's the moment of proposal that finally gets the girl. If yours is unclear, the outcome will be too.

The way to prepare the audience for your *culmination*, is to use the *pendulum* principle. As you may know, it takes a lot of effort to make a pendulum swing when it's at complete rest. However, when it's at the highest point of its swinging arc, only a small push is needed to get it moving back to the other side. This principle can be particularly effective in public speaking events where you are presenting solutions to difficulties. It's a matter of biological fact that our cerebral cortex happens to have more areas responsible for anxiety and fear than for pleasure. This is the reason behind the often-remarked fact that many people tend to focus more on the dangers and risks in life than the opportunities. It's also why newspapers and TV news programmes fill their schedules with war, violence, catastrophe and calamity – their bottom line is achieved by grabbing people's attention, and nothing does that like bad news and scary imagery. You can take advantage of this in the main body of your "problem-solving" presentation, by laying out all the problems your company is facing in graphic detail. For example, if you're giving a sales results presentation, you can talk about the difficulties and setbacks the company has faced. Talk as openly and frankly about the difficulties as you like, and break them down so that they are clear. Map out the setbacks and why they occurred. When the pendulum of the audience's mood is at its furthest extreme of negativity, you can then swoop in with your proposed solutions, and the sudden switch in emotion will make the culmination of your presentation even more effective.

Start by practising the pendulum principle with your relatives or friends. Once you get the hang of it and see how effective this technique is, you can use it to speak publicly.

By the way, up to 70% of commercials are created with the pendulum principle: first comes "the scare", then the "solution". To begin with, they tell you how harmful and painful root decay is, then they offer a bright solution in the form of a toothpaste. First, they draw a horrific picture of all the dangers that await you outside of your house, then they offer you a drinking yoghurt as protection. The protagonist feels unease in the morning, but after a refreshing and energising cup of some brand's tea, he's ready to face the day. Start by practising the pendulum principle with your relatives or friends. Once you get the hang of it and see how effective this technique is, you can use it to speak publicly.

In conclusion, I hope you all use the laws of composition wisely to your own and your audience's enjoyment!

FAQ Chapter Three

1

Dear Radislav, I have a couple of questions:

Is it possible to cover an issue in eight minutes? With regards to a scientific speech, how do you deliver a short message while making it significant and interesting, but without overloading it with complicated information?

If this is a scientific conference, then all the participants will get a pamphlet or booklet that has a summary of every report that is being introduced at the conference. That's where you should write the "complicated information". As for the performance, it's more of a presentation of the idea, rather than the published thesis itself, so it's important to make it brief and interesting, so that the participants will want to find and read your thesis. Plus, the ultimate goal of any conference is communication to its participants. Any speech or presentation given is a way of segmenting participants and giving them something to discuss. Of course, that's not the only goal, but every time I participated in a conference, I usually satisfied my vanity and made lots of new contacts.

What do you do when you have been preparing for a 15-minute speech but, right before your exit, you are told that, because of the large volume of performers, your time has been cut to 10 or even 8 minutes?

I have been in situations like that more than once. If you have used the Law of Composition that I always suggest to my listeners and readers, then you know you can widen or narrow down you speech to any size. In my trainings, I even have an exercise: participants get topics and prepare to speak but only find out how much time they have when they are on stage. Sometimes it's as short as 20 seconds. Try to do this on your own.

Ron Hoff, one of the few public speaking professionals that I respect, says that we should all shorten our performances to six minutes. In his book, "*Say It In Six*", published in 1996, he does slightly exaggerate – six minutes is probably a bit too short, but in general, he's right – speeches should and can be cut down.

2

Dear Radislav, is it true that, when you put someone else at the centre of attention in a group, you thus attract more attention to yourself? Thank you, Lena.

That's quite a catchphrase you have there. The kind Dale Carnegie would have wanted to come up with. But it is actually true – let's focus on the reason why. If there is a certain goal that you want to achieve by doing so and this kind of behaviour is a step towards it, that is understandable. But if it is done just for the hell of it, the people around will quickly figure it out. There is a great saying: "It is not enough to be right, it's important to be right at the right time." The tool you are describing is called "Inflating the Audience's Ego" and is used only at the first and fourth stages of communication. It's a bit complicated but I'll do my best to explain with a romantic analogy. Imagine yourself in bed with a woman. You begin to... er...

how do I put it... "make her the centre of attention". You're saying things like, "You are my only one. You are the prettiest of the prettiest." She obviously likes it. So you continue: "You drive me crazy, I can't sleep at night. You are in my head all the time. I have never met anybody like you." You go on like this for 20 minutes and suddenly realise that she's not feeling it anymore. But why? You're saying all these pleasant things, she is obviously the centre of your attention, what is the matter? The problem is that there's a time and a place for everything and, at some point, you have to move on to the next thing, otherwise your audience gets bored.

When you are communicating with the audience, you should say the main point of what you're trying to get across once you have created the appropriate emotional background for it. Otherwise, you might be accused of intellectual impotence.

This is why you should remember that the first (introduction) and fourth (conclusion) stages of communication should happen on a personal, emotional level, while the second and third, on logical and factual levels. You should talk business and not compliments there.

It will come with practice, don't worry.

3

Dear Radislav, I am fascinated with the "swinging pendulum" principle and people's reactions to it. I consciously imitated anger and hurt to stop a person's aggression towards me and it worked wonderfully. This person felt guilty and I easily convinced her of my point of view.

But to be completely frank, I think it's kind of deceitful to use psychological manipulation on people. I understand that politicians, the media and many others manipulate people into certain feelings but I can't help feeling it's wrong. What do you think? Looking forward to hearing your thoughts, Roman.

My opinion correlates with what Socrates once said: "If what you speak of is not the same as what's in your heart, nobody will believe you." Just like the Kama Sutra does not imitate the feelings of love, I never advise people to imitate their feelings. I have simply given you tools to fully express what you are feeling and an opportunity to achieve your goals. If you don't have goals yet, we can give you an opportunity to find them. This is true for any kind of practice: from tea ceremonies and astrology to languages, sports, painting and modelling.

I'm very happy to hear that the tools I've recommended worked. With practise, they can work miracles, and I myself have seen this happen many times. I don't know of a more powerful magic wand than speaking to people. Of course, you won't be able to make them do whatever you want – that would be *manipulation*, which is not my style, but you can persuade them to want what you need them to want, which would be *direction*. This skill of directing people and guiding them where you want is only mastered by the chosen few. These few decide that they accept the responsibility for the people they direct. This is a very hard but also very enjoyable process, and it would not work in any other way. Trust me.

4

Dear Radislav, I'm due to introduce my colleague in front of an audience by acknowledging his achievements. What should I include and how should I structure an intro like that? Thank you in advance, Oleg.

Oleg, regardless of what you say about yourself, any product or person you're introducing, the audience only wants to hear about things in a way that relates to themselves – they only want to know the pieces of information about the guy that you are introducing that will benefit them, e.g. what they can learn from him, what superior experience he has, etc.

Remember that the audience has a woman's psychology, even if it consists of only men. It wants to hear about itself. And if it doesn't, it loses interest both in the speaker and the person you are introducing.

There is such a thing as an "attention vector". It's important to direct it at the audience. How is this done? By constantly using the engagement technique, i.e. a live dialogue with the audience. Your speech needs to not only be about your colleague's achievements but also about how they may have affected or will affect the audience, even if it is only symbolically.

It's great if you can manage to get the audience into the shoes of the person that you are presenting. For example: "Imagine that you are a 10-year-old boy, thrown out on the streets of a city with no friends or family during the hungry post-war years. What would you say then if you were told that, in 20 years, you will become a sea captain..." and so on.

And the main thing: you are not dealing with facts, but rather with images of facts, so don't just use dates and numbers in your intro. Concentrate and present these facts in such a way that they will evoke feelings and emotions from the audience. It would also be a good idea to talk about feelings – what the person you're introducing is feeling and what the audience might feel in return.

Chapter Four

We have contact!

This chapter explains how to obtain and hold eye contact with your listeners and why it's important to do so skilfully.

And now let's talk about the one thing I'm really missing in this extended communication with you, my dear readers, which is eye contact. I don't think we need to get into too extended a description of why it's important, as it's something we've all experienced in all of our human interactions. However, if you really want to test it, try telling someone close to you "I love you" three times and compare their reactions. The first time, say it to them looking directly into their eyes. The second time – without looking at them at all. The third time – looking into someone else's eyes but not theirs.

To get all technical for a moment, it's critical not to underestimate the importance of a visual channel in the perception of a public appearance. After all, the optic nerve *is* 50 times thicker than the acoustic nerve. Through visual organs, we get over 90% of our information from the outside world. How you look at your audience is one of the key elements of the picture they perceive, and the impression of you they will get. They will read more from your eyes than your words.

Coming back to the idea that the audience's behaviour is similar to that of a woman, you need to remind yourself of how a woman would react if you didn't give her enough attention. She would get offended and you might very well end up sleeping on the couch. The same goes for your listeners; they will drift and your words will be lost in the ether if there's nothing holding you and them together. They see a trace of profound interest in your eyes, a silent question – do you like what I'm saying and how I'm saying it? – but to achieve this, you need to be interested in your listeners too, and the easiest way to express that interest is with eye contact.

Here's an example of eye contact being neglected. I recently went to a concert by a famous Belarusian rock group, Okean Elzy. Although the concert was held in an intimate venue, the singer spent the whole gig gazing over the heads of the audience, staring at the microphone or at the ceiling. It felt like he was avoiding everyone's eyes. Needless to say, the rest of the band just stared down at their instruments. It seemed like the whole group were basically absent. The music was great but why did the applause vanish so quickly? Where was the screaming until people were hoarse? Where were the stamping feet and swelling roars of "More, more, MORE !!" Why did no teenage fan spend a night crying over the love letter to the guy on stage that would never be sent? In other words, with the other constants in this equation unchanged, but with a skilful use of eye contact, the effect would have been a lot stronger. I only mentioned Okean Elzy because my memories of that night are still fresh. Anybody could have been in their shoes. I guarantee I can prove my thesis and triple how much applause any band can get (and quadruple the amount of love letters).

What comes first?

First things first: once you've found your place on stage, don't rush straight into your speech; remember the emotional ambiance you have to create first. We have covered how to do that with words, phrases and introductory speech in the previous chapter; now I'd like to look at the equally important but often overlooked matter of body language.

Start by having a mildly benevolent expression on your face, but don't overdo the smile because it will seem artificial. American textbooks on communication are great but if you follow their advice and stretch your mouth into one of those wide million-dollar white teeth smiles, your audience will expect an over-the-top sales pitch, which is not your goal. Stuff like that may have worked in the past, but audiences these days are much more aware of the "tricks of the trade", and are more likely to react and connect with a natural and positive look. So keep a cheerful, light and genuine look while carefully glancing over your audience. Go from person to person, pausing a moment at all, or almost all of them. If you happen to catch a friendly smile, give them a barely noticeable nod as if to say, "Oh, hello, you're here too? How lovely to see you!", even if you're seeing this person for the first time in your life. Next, imagine you are stretching invisible threads from here to yourself. Later, you will use these to keep their attention while you speak. Only after you have established this eye contact with every individual person in the room can you proceed with your speech. I want to emphasise that I am not talking about scanning over the whole audience but about looking each person in the eye. I predict a question: what if the room you're talking to is too big or the lights that are shining at you make you go temporarily blind? Then you simply imitate eye contact. For instance, a ballet dancer appears on stage and pauses for a moment while looking the audience over from left to right, only after which does she go into her first steps. Of course, the stage lights are too bright for her to see anybody's head in the audience, let alone their eyes, but the audience is left with the feeling that she has looked into the soul of each one of them and is now dancing just for their individual pleasure.

To temporarily slip from the language of love to the language of war, you can say that establishing eye contact is the equivalent of a drone-guided surgical strike, as opposed to carpet-bombing. I often hear people say that it would take too much time to do all this, but the simple answer is, no, it won't. Even if you only give each person a fraction of a second, this process will still be meaningful and will go by much quicker than you expect. Don't try to establish eye contact with the audience as a whole; pick each person individually. First, establish eye contact with the people who are already looking at you (some might even smile back), then slowly, move to the ones that are usually occupied with their own business – get them to look at you and they will never dare to look away for the rest of your speech. Wait for the rest of the audience to look at you so that there isn't anybody in the audience who's not paying attention to what's happening on stage. This is important for the success of the whole speech. Imagine that there are cables attaching your eyes to the eyes of the audience members and that the information you are trying to get across in your speech is flowing through them. Imagine that the eye contact that you have creates a constant force-field that contains all the information that's transferred from you to the audience, and if this force-field gets damaged or interrupted, the information flow will stop. And if these cables are cut, the current of information stops as well. (Actually, that's not too fanciful a metaphor – that is almost how it really happens.) The same thing happens when speaking to a friend: eye contact ensures that the information that is being exchanged is getting through and is being registered by the person listening. Knowing that you are not only "listened" to, but "heard" is paramount. But eye contact with the audience is a two-way street; you, as the speaker, get something in return as well. You obtain information on whether the message is being understood or something needs to be repeated, whether the audience is tired and may need a break, whether the subject is interesting or you might want to move forward – all these are things you can learn from your audience while maintaining eye contact with them.

Reaching the "neglected" and where to stand

The most neglected parts of the audience in terms of establishing eye contact are usually seated on the balcony (last rows) and on the sides (far left and far right). It is from them that you get the toughest questions or you can hear people coughing, chatting, or fiddling with pens and mobile phones. Why? The simple answer is that we don't reach them or pay enough attention to the people who are sitting in those seats, because they are simply too far away or awkwardly placed. The sector of visibility of an experienced public speaker is 40 to 45 degrees, and 30 to 35 degrees for a beginner. This unfortunately means that a novice speaker's eyes can stay fixed on the centre portion of the audience and end up only communicating with them. In this case, it's only the people who are sitting there, nodding and laughing at your jokes, who are listening to every word. The rest of the audience may as well have gone home.

So how does the speaker position himself on stage so that eye contact with the whole of the audience is established? Since there is a great number of differently shaped and sized rooms, I can give you a rule that would work best in a rectangular-shaped room, but is also applicable to any other shape or size. Basically, you need to find a point that would form the apex of an equilateral triangle between you and the persons sitting at the extreme left and extreme right of the front rows. Make sure it is an equilateral triangle and not an isosceles. This is your ideal distance for creating the preliminary eye contact. Follow this rule and you will easily be able to figure out where on stage to start your speech. I am only talking about beginning your speech there, because after you do, you will want to start moving around the stage, maybe coming closer to the edge or further away from it, going where the rhythm takes you.

Quick Note

Make sure to pay attention to the corners of the room where you hear movement, noise, whispering or snoring – this could mean that the connection is broken and you need to quickly fix it. Communicate with those who are deprived of your eye contact, come closer and address them with a question, let them understand that you are waiting to hear an answer from them specifically. Trust me; this will get their attention back almost instantly. By constantly keeping eye contact throughout your speech, we keep these "high-risk" groups in check, making sure they are fully engaged in what you're saying. Under no circumstances should you lose this contact. You may look away for an instant to show a chart or glance at a note, but no more than that. Follow the news anchors' lead – they only glance away from the camera for a fraction of a second. When looking at the audience, even if you lose your train of thought for a moment and forget what you wanted to say, your gaze will help you through it and make it seem like the pause was intentional, giving whatever words come out of your mouth a sense of added wisdom. At the same time, you don't want to turn your speech into a creepy group hypnosis session – keep it natural, don't keep your head too still, and look at different people in the audience.

FAQ Chapter Four

1

Dear Radislav, I am having some difficulties with speaking into the microphone on stage because I can't see the eyes of my audience and so I can't establish contact. I have a seminar for 150 people next week, what can I do? Thank you, Olga.

Pretend. "Imagine" the people in the room and work with them like there is a contact. I have been in these kinds of situations frequently – and all ended well. It would probably be good for your peace of mind though if you can make sure that the contact is definitely there, so try provoking some applause or exclamations from your audience.

2

Dear Radislav, can you please tell me how to perform in front of an imaginary audience, i.e. speaking into a camera. I need to record a couple of training sessions for an online audience and this is my first time. How do I do it when there's no human contact. Thanks a lot, Varia.

The way to solve this is to sit a couple of your friends or family behind the camera. This way, you get the human contact, reaction, feedback and support that you need. But try to remember that your *main* audience is the viewer, so all attention should be on them.

3

Dear Radislav, whenever I teach, I usually always make eye contact with my students. It happens automatically and effortlessly. But recently I have noticed one peculiar thing – if I'm explaining new and complicated material, I tend to look at the students that are "stronger", and if I'm talking about mistakes and potential errors, I look at the "weaker" students. I haven't yet decided whether that's bad or not, so I would like to hear your opinion. Thank you very much, Natalia.

A famous author once wrote, *"You look like the best and the worst person in the world... because they are all the same people."* What I mean is – there are no "stronger" or "weaker" students, and I say this as a former teacher. You can confirm that simply by changing a teacher in a class and see that the students' grades will change accordingly. I once had a student who had spent a while in a juvenile prison – and within a couple of months, I had him fall in love with classical literature and analysing it the way a college sophomore majoring in linguistics would. Or a football scholarship student who read the two volumes of "War and Peace" cover to cover. I am not saying this to brag, but only to emphasise my point: there is no such thing as a weak student – a lot depends on the teacher and his perception of the student in question.

The next time you talk about potential errors or mistakes, try looking at those who you think are "strong", and when you explain the complicated, new material, try looking at those who you considered "weak". But don't just look at them, make sure they understand what you're saying and participate. Then observe their reactions to this, maybe suggest that they solve the new, complicated material, ask for their opinion on the topic, etc. And make sure you are genuinely interested in how they respond. Maybe take time after the lesson to discuss the lecture with one of them. I promise that in a few weeks you will be amazed by the change – but try not to neglect you straight-A students either.

4

Dear Radislav, how can I handle speaking in front of a small group of people with my friends present? Through the people that I know, I usually try to establish a friendlier contact with the whole group, but I really don't want to give my attention only to them, thus dividing the audience. Maybe I shouldn't pay too much attention to my friends, but then won't they get offended? Please tell me what you think, Artur.

Usually, when choosing a method of interacting with the audience, a speaker would work on the basis of the question: "What's reasonable?". That's why he shouldn't pay too much attention to what relatives/friends/acquaintances think about him. However, I must say that we often overestimate the sensitivity of the people close to us. Remember that your friends probably understand that you have a responsibility before your audience and that expecting too much of your attention is silly. In addition to that, if the audience knows that your friends are in the room and they notice you paying them more attention than to everyone else, you will get in trouble. The audience gets jealous very quickly; they may forgive a lot of things but not this. I have said before that it has a female psychology, and women can't stand indifference. But there can be only one thing that's worse than indifference – when some other woman gets more attention. You can probably draw the final conclusions on your own.

5

Dear Radislav, I can't really understand how to make eye contact with all of the 30 people sitting in front of me; won't they think that I'm a weirdo, having gathered everyone in a room just to stare at them. So what should I do? A roll call doesn't always help, especially when it comes to peculiar names that are difficult to pronounce. Thanks a lot, Vadim.

OK. First of all, one second per person is too much; it can and should be much quicker than that. Secondly, a long, establishing eye contact is needed only when:

- the audience is very large
- the audience is lacking concentration
- you came to announce something very important and you need complete attention
- the reason of your speech is festive or sad
- your presentation was highly-anticipated
- you yourself are very nervous and feel that it's hard to begin without a pause

- your speech was announced but the battery in the mic died and now you're waiting for it to be changed.

Thirdly, you need to establish eye contact with each listener, not with the whole audience. As I say in my trainings, establishing eye contact is not about "mass bombing", it's about "precision strikes". You don't shift your glance from person to person but rather pick them from different sectors of the room. This is hard to demonstrate in an email.

And, finally, a roll call is no help at all. It's reminiscent of army or jail and is used to check who's missing and punish the absentees. Also, you're right – both you and people with unusual names will feel silly and embarrassed if you pronounce their names incorrectly, which will have the others laughing. Seems to me that this is not how you would want your speech to begin.

CHAPTER FIVE

Let Your Body Do The Talking...

This chapter exposes exactly how vital the speaker's posture is for both speaker and audience. I'll also discuss gesticulation and other movements during your appearance.

We often underestimate the importance of a speaker's posture. The importance here is not only in how we look but also in how we feel. To get technical for a moment, it is important to understand that all the muscles in the human body are wired to certain areas of the cerebral cortex. It is this part of our brain that tells our muscles to flex or relax, depending on what's going on in our environment. If we are scared, we shrink, lift our shoulders up and step back. If we are having fun, we fling our arms and tilt our head back. If we feel aggressive, we tend to bend forward, let our chin drop, etc. The very interesting thing about all this is that the connection between muscles and the brain is actually a two-way street. Although the muscle-flexing usually happens as a response to a feeling, it has now been demonstrated that if we flex certain groups of muscles, we can help to induce certain feelings at will. If you are in a bad mood, try forcing yourself to smile for five minutes. You will soon notice you feel a lot better. Another example; many people in Arabic countries eat with their legs crossed. It's impossible to start running when you are in this position, so the use of this posture sends a signal to the brain saying: "Everything is OK, I'm not in any danger, I can relax." Your brain and body can concentrate on digesting the food that comes in.

So what's the best position for us to adopt, that will not only look good but also send our brain the right signals? Stand with your feet about 20 to 25 centimetres apart, spread your toes a little and put one slightly in front of the other (your leading leg behind you). Your centre of gravity should be shifted slightly forward. Your shoulders should be lowered and relaxed. Your spine is straight. You should lift your chin slightly. If you feel some constraint in your body, move a little and try looking for a position in which you are comfortable. It is important to have a little bit of everything but not to go to extremes. The toes are slightly spread apart, the centre of gravity is shifted a little, etc. There should be nothing tense or fake about this pose. Did it work? Great! This is the right position! Classic.

What does this position do to us? What does our body tell our brain in this situation? "I am calm. I am confident in myself. I know what I am talking about." It's important to constantly be aware of your centre of gravity. If it is shifted forward, this is the position of an outgoing person, prepared to make a move and insist on his or her point of view. If we shift it backwards, this becomes the position of a person who is ready to retreat (both physically and away from his or her point of view), of someone who is not sure of himself and ready to obey. An unknown force transmits these signals, not only to our brain but also to the public. The public wants to see a leader in a public speaker, someone who embodies strength. The way a woman looks at a man. The way you stand, if it fits this profile, will be a powerful signal to the audience. Having said that, there are some times when you can relax and "pull back" a little – like the moments in your presentation when you open the floor to the audience response.

But even here, don't overdo it: don't turn into a statue up there. It's very difficult for people to concentrate on what you're saying if you're too still, so please move around, keeping in mind the classic pose. You can do whatever movement feels natural within that classic pose, even sit. But you need to begin and then return to it during your speech. Make sure your movements are unrestrained and relaxed. Coming back to the ballet dancer example, remember that, when he appears on stage, he assumes the same position but slightly exaggerated: his back is straight, his centre of gravity is shifted forward, his chin is up and shoulders are wide. Whichever movement he goes into, he always returns to this position and starts from it.

Your posture also influences the tempo and the intonation of your voice; another non-content factor that plays a huge part in the success or otherwise of your presentation. You need to practise this to get it right. Find the position that is most comfortable for you. Maybe try moving your feet a little closer to each other or bending your back less and you will see that everything will fall into place. After you've assumed the position that works best for you, try rehearsing your speech; you should really feel the difference at this point.

At my training sessions, we often do an interesting exercise that helps my students memorise the position that they need to stand in during the speech. This means they don't have to concentrate on posture while they're on stage, freeing them up to be much more natural, as the correct position comes automatically. You, my dear readers, can practise this on your own too. Firstly, find the position in which you feel comfortable and, once you've got it, close your eyes and imagine yourself as if you're a mould for making tin soldiers. Freeze in this position, feel the molten metal rising and rising, filling you up to the crown of your head. When the tin fills you up, blow on it so that it cools down. Remain in the position of a "tin orator" for a few seconds. Now relax, exhale, and open your eyes. That's it. Your body has now memorised this position and you don't need to think about it while performing. My congratulations!

What do you do with your hands?

Gesticulation is a very individual thing, and varies from person to person, but there are definitely some universals that are worth exploring. Let's start by thinking of the early years of cinema at the beginning of the 20th century. Why do you think actors made those over-the-top grimaces and did so much exaggerated hand-wringing? Why did they have such ridiculous makeup? Why were their movements so exaggerated? The answer is that most of those early cinema actors had started out in theatre. Back then, theatre stages were not as well-lit as they are now, so the melodramatic, expressive gestures were necessary, otherwise the audience would not have seen anything at all.

It's worth remembering this little fact when we are thinking about our body language. Even though the rooms where you will be speaking are likely to be well-lit to the modern standards, you must keep in mind the size of the room and its different distractions. To keep the audience's attention, you need to turn your normal gestures into powerful communicative tools, and to do that, you will have to gesticulate much more actively than you do in your everyday life. The typical range of gestures in a face-to-face conversation is roughly to the diameter of a basketball. However, when you're standing in a room with a large audience, you'll have to use the same gestures but cover a space with a diameter of about six foot! That is how expansive your gestures should be – and don't be afraid to look silly. Your audience genuinely won't feel like anything out of the ordinary is happening.

Make sure that every gesture you make gets fully developed. If you start moving your arm to the right, make sure your extend it completely, including your wrist and fingers. Open movements and open palms reassures the audience that you have nothing to hide and are open to them. Be careful of the gesture I've christened: "What money?!" I once saw a couple of motivational videos made by a renowned Russian businessman, Vladimir Dovgan, for his company's distributor representatives. These short films are very well done – he has great tempo, visual aids, body language, and an overall energetic feel. But there was one in particular that really struck the wrong chord. Throughout this film, his hand is not open, but almost curled up into a fist, as if he's holding or hiding something in it. After a while, I started to get the feeling that the speaker was holding information back from me – the viewer. Of course, I can't say for sure that he was holding something back – but that's certainly the impression he gave. Other people that have seen the videos felt the same, although they couldn't explain why, it was only an unconscious feeling. I knew it instantly, because it's my job to know. And I wanted you to see how a small detail like that can ruin a brilliant speech. So keep your palms open; remember that all greeting gestures are made with an open palm – handshake, wave, blessing, salute – because they are welcoming and safe.

Relax...

A typical problem is constrained gesticulation. It's usually what happens in an attempt to suppress anxiety. However, the other extreme of this suppression is excessive movement. For instance, rumour has it that a famous Russian actress, Marina Neelova, was so nervous at her graduation performance in theatre school that she actually fell right off the stage. Jerky, out-of-place movements that don't seem to be fully under your control will always subtly present themselves as signs of anxiety to your audience. Accompanied by a nervous, shifting glance, paleness and irregular breathing, you will quickly become the perfect picture of someone with no confidence in themselves at all. To fight this phenomenon, re-read the chapter on suppressing anxiety.

Even if you don't consciously feel anxious, it's surprising how many of us are constantly making slight nervous twitches with our hands or even face. We can even sometimes find ourselves pacing back and forth, back and forth, like a dog that has been chained. I interpret these moments as your body asking for movement. If you were a horse, you'd be pawing the ground right about now. So you need to fulfil this need by starting to move around consciously and in a controlled fashion. With time, gesticulation, any movement on stage will become natural and anxiety-free. Overall, try to move more. This attracts attention and helps relieve tension, not to mention that the impression you will give is of a motivated person, full of energy.

To round off this topic, I will describe an **exercise that helps eliminate non-functional gesticulation** (if you have chronic problems with this). For the exercise, you will need yourself, a big mirror, and a couple of volumes of the *Encyclopaedia Britannica*. Stand in front of the mirror, holding one volume in your left hand and the other in your right. Now repeat the speech you have prepared. From time to time, you will find your hands automatically trying to make gestures – these are the functional ones that you definitely need to keep in your repertoire. The heaviness of the books will automatically restrain the non-functional, non-essential gestures.

It is also important here to note one thing that may not be instantly obvious. Have you ever paid attention to what time different wristwatches on TV ads are showing? As a rule, it is usually ten minutes to two or ten minutes past ten. Why? When the hands are in this position, it reminds us of a smile and makes us think positively. When the hands are pointing down, like they would at, let's say, twenty past four, this reminds us of the downturned corners of the mouth that we see when someone is sad. This feeling is unconsciously passed along to the potential buyer and forms a certain attitude towards the product that is being advertised. Alas, we often give away our true feelings about what we are saying by directing all of our gestures towards the ground, unconsciously hinting at negativity. Make sure to pay attention to this and you will know I am right. Does this mean that when we are gesticulating we should always be lifting our hands up? Not always. As we know now, there are moments (during the *main part* of the speech) when we *should* show the audience our concern or dissatisfaction with the problems, maybe even provoke their anger. This is a perfect place for gestures facing down. Observe a few public speakers at meetings. When they greet the public, their gestures are directed upwards, when they are debunking authorities, they shake their finger, shake their fist, and dissect the air with their palm – and all of these movements are directed down. When it's time to call for action, the gestures are elevated again. Now it's the *conclusion* of the speech – a time for uniting gestures when your arms are almost prepared to embrace the audience. And this, again, is up. Never forget that our gestures influence the audience and ourselves, regardless of whether we realise it or not.

Hands in pockets

I know there are a few people out there who sew up their trouser pockets to avoid the temptation to put their hands there. This, of course, is an extreme measure. It is, however, an interesting question – hands in pockets? Overall, I don't really see anything wrong with putting your hands in your pockets from time to time – one or even both. I actually do it myself sometimes as well. Of course, this is only appropriate during casual moments – and it still probably isn't a "one size fits all" thing – you'll just have to figure out if it works for you. Once, I suggested that one of my clients should hold his left hand in his pants pocket during certain parts of the speech. He needed to do it for three reasons: to feel more casual, to get rid of the non-functional wrist movements, and also to compensate for the status and age differences between him and the audience. That was just one of the many cases I've come across. However, there are many situations in which leaving your hands in your pockets is unacceptable. Everything depends on the type of event you're participating in. Don't do it at the very beginning and the conclusion of a speech. Definitely not when receiving an honour from the Queen, when reading an obituary, or when toasting newly-weds. I'm sure you can easily figure out which situations are "non-pocket" situations. And so you can see there are no set rules on this particular issue – it's best to go with what feels natural, as any effort to "force" yourself to follow a rule will result in unnatural straining. It is always important for me to know how a person feels. At my trainings and individual sessions, I always ask my clients whether they are feeling OK, *what* they're feeling, does everything feel comfortable, etc. In the end, I would like to urge you to try and figure out what comes naturally to you and go with that. Practise the exercises in this chapter and your body language will speak louder than words and embellish your speech.

FAQ Chapter Five

1

Dear Radislav, the posture of a public speaker is very important when the speaker is standing centre stage where everybody can see him. But if the speaker is forced to talk from behind a stand and is visible only from the chest up – what then? Should a classic pose be assumed or is there a different but comfortable way to stand? Thank you in advance, Sergey.

Like I said before, the posture is less important for the audience than it is to the speaker. The way you stand, the confidence that you project, the tone of your voice that you use, all those things will in turn influence the audience. If you assume the classic posture, everything will fall into place and you will be listened to.

2

Dear Radislav, I wasn't very tall when I was younger and had to deliver my thesis from behind a lectern. It was way too high for me and I could hardly reach the microphone. I didn't lose my cool, however, I just adjusted the mic so that I was heard and said, "You might not see me, but you will hear me clearly", and delivered my speech. It went very successfully that time! Since then, I have grown and learned to wear heels, so my height is no longer a problem, but still, if again asked to speak from behind a lectern, can I refuse to use it without looking too much of a prima donna? Let me know what you think, Irina.

I actually always recommend that people don't use lecterns if they can help it. The audience is mostly affected by what they see, but when you are standing behind a lectern, you are limiting your ability to affect them via the main channel – visually. You also can't really move around from behind a stand – and as you know, moving objects get more attention and focus than static ones, so it's silly to deprive yourself of that. Keep in mind another thing – the place from which you are speaking is very important, because if the speaker before you stood behind a lectern and bored the audience for three hours, you will have an extremely difficult time "waking" them up from that same lectern. In that case, it's better to not use the stand but move around the stage.

3

Dear Radislav, what should I do if I am suddenly asked to join someone on stage for an impromptu participation in a speech? Imagine I am mentally prepared and confident of my subject, but my outfit is not appropriate and really singles me out from all the speakers. I remember you saying that the audience remembers mostly what they see, so is it better to avoid coming on stage in this situation or should I continue as I am and hope that my words will win them over? Thank you, Masha.

This is a situation where the best choice is for the lesser evil. Obviously, dashing out of the room will look comical. I remember participating once in a big, international conference on the eve of Perestroika in the 90s. It was organised in a posh, five-star hotel with a large number of foreign guests and the local administration. Everyone was wearing ties and suits and looked very official, decked out in their finest. Then suddenly, the host introduced to the stage the head of the Kyiv Literary Institute and he came up wearing a white sweat-suit and trainers with no speech prepared. Instantly, everyone stopped what they were doing and turned to listen with interest, precisely because he looked the way he did and it aroused curiosity. He began speaking confidently without being apologetic for his outfit, and in fact, it was the people in the audience who felt uneasy and a little overdressed. His speech was successful; he even went on to become a minister. And one editor-in-chief of a popular magazine back then said: "You might eat with your hands in the most expensive restaurant, and it will look like nothing out of the ordinary, as long as you don't start to apologise for it." Do you see what I mean, Masha?

4

Dear Radislav, I need to consult you on a rather peculiar subject. I was wondering if it's OK to, say, take off a jacket or a cardigan during a performance to make yourself more comfortable. Or is it better not to distract the audience by taking a layer off? Thanks for your reply, Yulia.

It is perfectly normal to take off a jacket or something similar during a speech. I once attended a training in Amsterdam by a very famous coach, Paul Storimans. At the beginning of his speech he took off his jacket, then later, undid his tie, then unbuttoned the top of his shirt. After the first half, he took the tie off completely and rolled up his sleeves. I don't know what else he would have taken off if the seminar had gone for any longer. I can't say that I remember what he was saying, but I do remember *how* he was doing it. You see, several mechanisms go to work here: the first one is that moving objects attract more attention, and the second is breaking a stereotype, which is always an attention-grabber.

Furthermore, I think that, at this point, our primal instincts come into play as well. Imagine, a young woman speaker taking her cardigan off in front of a room full of men; she doesn't undress completely of course, but a man's imagination goes a long way...

5

Dear Radislav, I have two questions. How do you hold back the giggles while performing? And also, what do you do when you need to hide your anger from the audience? Hope to hear your thoughts, Igor.

You need to tightly press your tongue against where the roof of your mouth meets your teeth. And if you're trying to hold back your anger, you should put all your weight on your tip-toes and push them firmly on the ground.

CHAPTER SIX

Perfect Timing

This chapter uses vivid examples to explain when to show your audience graphs, slides, posters, and any other visuals.

When do you show the pretty stuff?

As we have already noted, the ocular nerve of the human body is 50 times thicker than the hearing nerve. So when speaking publicly, always think about what can be shown rather than described verbally. The actual object that you're talking about, its copy, pictures, graphs, charts, drawings, photos, maps, etc. Visual aids bring in diversity, help retain attention and make the speech more memorable.

Multimedia projectors are used very frequently to enhance a speech or a performance. The slides are created as a PowerPoint, or a Key Note presentation (or a similar app), the pictures are digitalised, and sometimes, different elements such as videos or animation are inserted. That's all straightforward and very well-known. The speaker can control the slides or set them to be changed automatically at a certain interval. The thing to remember here is that, when you arrange the material for your visual presentation, make sure that the order creates the powerful and positive emotional tension that you need. Only dim the lights instead of turning them off completely to give people the opportunity to write things down.

From the moment you start showing slides, they begin "to speak for you", which in turn partially solves the problem of eye contact and gesticulation, if you're having problems with it. Of course, the audience will *still* see you, so don't go grimacing or gurning at them. Also, try to cut down on the expressive hand gestures at this point, and think of yourself simply as a voiceover. If you stick to the same expansiveness of gesture while the slides are on, you'll just end up looking like a crazy person, gesticulating in the dark. Having said that, it is really important that you don't turn your presentation into a mere commentary of the slides – any slideshows need to be interspersed with moments where the focus is on you – in which you'll naturally be expressive and expansive.

Technicality

Introducing the visual aids is a sensitive issue. Show them only when they are genuinely relevant to your speech and when they enhance it. They should not be on the screen or hung up in advance, and need to be removed or turned off as soon as you have finished talking about them. If you keep a slide on the screen that is no longer being discussed, your audience will have a hard time concentrating on what you are saying. I suggest that, when preparing a slideshow, you leave every other slide blank, not white, but with a background that is a generic version of your slideshow (without text or pictures). That way, if you need to have a little detour before the next slide, you have this generic slide to tide you over, and if you don't, you simply double-click on you mouse and move on without anyone even noticing the blank slide. This is a perfect solution for situations like this and avoids confusing the audience or drawing too much unnecessary attention to itself.

It's a given that, when you're doing a slideshow, the possibility of eye contact is very limited. Still, there is something you can do that doesn't involve them looking at you – you can use your voice. Take more pauses, change the tempo of your voice, ask the audience questions ("Isn't that so?" "Doesn't that sound familiar?"). Don't think about eye contact right now, you will still have time for it during your brilliant finale with the lights on.

There are a few things about putting a visual presentation together that define a professional and, if you follow a few simple rules, you won't fall into the category of an amateur.

- **Three colours.** Now, it's clear that the more colourful, the better. However, you will have to limit your imagination to using only three colours when you are making slides. A larger number of colours is not only a bit tacky, but also distracts from registering the information clearly. One quick note though: I'm not talking about colour photography, because those colours are limitless.

- **One style.** It's best to have the slides made in one style. To do that, use the same template. If you are making a presentation for your own company or on its behalf, the template should feature the company logo and a background with the company colours. This should be done in muted tones so as not to distract the eye too much.

- **Three Fonts.** There are limitations with fonts too. Try not to use more than three. Italics would be considered a separate font. On the first slide, I suggest you put the title of your speech and your name (you can add the date if it's important to the presentation). The last slide should be in a smaller font, stating the title of your presentation and, again, your full name (no initials) and contact details.

A quick point I'll make about technology in general: we often have far too much faith in it, and the idea that it might fail on us seems unlikely. People tell themselves that, at the presentation, they will easily be able to operate a piece of equipment, never having seen or used it before. As a result, everything blows up in smoke and the speaker is looking at chaos he can't possibly fix. It's either the lights that won't switch off or on when they need to, or the music that won't play one minute but then comes on randomly while the speaker is talking, and it's either too loud or too quiet, or it's the mic that begins to squeak as soon as you turn it on – the potential for chaos is endless. To avoid all these calamities, you simply need to have a final run-through, a dress rehearsal, if you will. This will give you time to make sure everything is working in the room that you're scheduled to appear in. You can even do it several times, to be absolutely certain. If you have an assistant, have him or her remember the sequence of events, and be on standby if something should go wrong. If you are a thorough person and like to have "all exits" covered, rehearse for the scenarios where something goes south – such as the lights going off, or the projector not working, the CD player shutting down, and so on.

How should I put this?

It would be great if, during your presentation, you can show the audience the actual product (or something that is the topic of your speech). But be careful to not overdo it, and think about the logistics, because even in what seems to be a simple set-up, there can be drawbacks. A long time ago, before cell phones existed, when "beepers" and pagers were introduced in Russia for the first time, I took part in a presentation for a communications company, where the organisers brought in a giant, inflatable pager to show the audience. It was too big for the room so they put it in the garden, which was a bad idea because it distracted the listeners as it swayed in the wind. The most awkward moment was when one person asked: "What is it?" and the poor speakers couldn't find anything better to reply but "Well, it's a pager, it's a tiny little thing and you carry it around..." In the end, the only thought that the audience was left with was that this "pager thingy" is a giant, inflatable scam. Funnily enough, none of the organisers of this introduction had a real pager to show the audience.

The important tool to understand and use if necessary is this – if you have nothing "real" to show the audience, try to create an image using visually-enhanced verbs. Something like this: "*Imagine* this...", "Let's *observe*...", "Let's *reflect* for a moment...", "Try to *recall* the last time...", "What if we *focused* on..." This should be accompanied by active gesticulation as well. It should be enhancing the creation of these mental images. I call this "*gesticulated visualisation*". For instance, you say, "Just think about it! Last year, this number was at 20,000 points; this year, it is 40,000; next year, we expect a growth of up to 100,000 points." These words should be accompanied, not merely by the waving of hands, but a pantomime where you try to show the height of an imaginary poll at 20,000, then at 40,000, then reaching up to 100,000. To try this out on your own, and make sure you understand the basic principle, try to visualise the following phrases with gestures : "Let's try to imagine how we went from a tiny family business to a giant corporation." "The train is going from point A to point B." "The water goes into the pool through one tube and comes out of the other." Got it?

If you want to increase the visual effect even more, spice up your speech with energetic verbs of movement. Here are just a few examples of dynamic imagery you can use to give your presentation a sense of energy:

- Problems *came up* → Problems *arose*; we *were faced* with difficulties

- The project was successful → The project *was heading* for success

- Our meeting is over → Our meeting *has come to* an end

- Our target *was* → We *aimed* to

You – the object

The most important visual object is, of course, you – and you should never forget that! This is where everything matters and, as strange as it may seem, the smaller the detail, the bigger the role it plays in your appearance. I recently took part in a serious research project into the importance of tie colour and width in a presenter's outfit. Don't laugh – the study showed how participants who took part in this focus group often failed to remember whether the speaker was bald or had hair, or was wearing glasses or not; but they could easily remember small details such as that their socks were pink, or their stockings were sagging, a hair was out of place, or a bra was visible through a blouse and so on.

Of course, there are some details that go without saying, like shaving, polishing shoes, ironing shirts and so on. I'm going to assume that most of my readers are on top of those. I now move on to summarise some of the less obvious things you can do to get things right visually:

- **Grimace.** Spend two minutes on the morning of your presentation in front of a mirror. In that time, actively grimace and hold each face for no more than four seconds. Make the most ridiculous faces and have fun with it! This will warm up facial muscles, stimulate blood circulation, and make your face more expressive and flexible. As an added bonus, your face will look fitter and healthier. This is very important. Your audience must see a healthy, energetic, powerful and confident person. It works better than words. You may want to include grimacing as part of your morning ritual, somewhere in between brushing your teeth and shaving.

- **No lecture stands.** I would always recommend that you don't use a (free-standing) lecture stand. As I have mentioned before, the audience reacts to what they see; when you stand behind a stand, you are much less active and expressive, thus the visual channel for influencing your audience is shut down. You can't really move behind it; it's like you're glued to it and, as I said, static objects attract far less attention than moving ones. The other thing to remember is that the audience associates with the place from which you are speaking to them. In other words, if there was a long and monotonous lecture given from behind that lecture stand right before you, then you will have a difficult time breaking the already-formed stereotype if you give your speech from that same place. On the other hand, if there was a fun and engaging appearance and the audience feels energetic and eager to listen, then you can use the stand to your advantage, although, I should say that, even then, you'll need to begin to move around the stage as soon as you can.

- **Outfit.** The audience always looks attentively at what the speaker is wearing and draws their own conclusions, often unconsciously – this means you should be careful when deciding on an outfit. The audience is always slightly suspicious of a speaker who comes up on stage dressed too extravagantly. It's acceptable if they know you well or if it jump-starts an interesting intrigue, a move, or a challenge that you will skilfully use during the speech. I applaud that. Taking your jacket off, rolling up your sleeves, loosening your tie – any transformation in your clothing may have the most powerful effect on the audience, and leave a long-lasting impression. I enjoy watching things like that, but only when it's done by aces of public speaking. If you're a newbie, I advise you to stay away from experiments, and put them off until you have fully mastered what is written in this book. Before then, you might have a hard time speaking if your outfit is too flashy, unless you're working in the fashion industry. Obviously, context is everything – know your crowd, feel the room and choose your outfit accordingly.

- **Friend or Foe details.** I have already mentioned the "friend or foe" tool in chapter three, but I want to return to it for a second to explain how it can be applicable here. You might have heard of a "friend or foe" identification gadget on military defence planes. Every plane and every ground control has one, so when a plane is flying over the ground, ground control sends a message asking if the plane is a "friend". The on-board gadget then responds with "friend". An enemy's plane would send a signal, interpreted as "foe", and be shot down. Human brains are equipped with similar "gadgets" that help us identify menaces. We analyse everybody we come in contact with, based on parameters such as these: "How much like myself is he/she? How much of myself is there in him/her?" In other words, "Is this person a friend or foe?" Obviously, we are more willing to trust and listen to a person who looks like us, or has similar interests. For instance, a conversation will quickly move forward if both people in it are smokers and can have a cigarette together, or if both people ride bikes to work, or go to the same gym, etc. It gets even better if they prefer the same brand of clothing, were born in the same city, or went to the same school. Whatever problem or issue there was would quickly find a solution if people connect over something they have in common.

Imagine a young woman, walking down a dark alley (these things do still happen). A slightly older man appears and comes up to her. He is unshaved, wearing a sweatshirt and old, ripped shoes. He has a tattoo on his left hand and is gripping something tightly behind his back in his right hand. A hushed sound of a bird fluttering somewhere in the trees echoes in the night. A lonely reflection falls on the blade behind the man's back, and leaves no doubt what he is about to do. Hiding his true intentions, he says to her, "Hey baby, get undressed, I have a surprise for you." The woman sprints away down the street as fast as she can, screaming, "Help! Help! Anyone!" When she gets to her house, she's too frightened and can't find her keys to open the front door, so she rings the doorbell. A man opens the door – he is an unshaven man with a tattoo, an apron, and a knife that he is awkwardly trying to hide behind his back. "Why are you out of breath? Take off your coat, I have a surprise for you." This time, the woman doesn't run away screaming for help; on the contrary, she breathes a sigh of relief and follows her husband, safe in the knowledge that the knife is not intended for her but to cut the delicious pie he has cooked for dinner. Notice how both situations and the words are almost identical, but the only difference is the source: whether he's a friend or a foe.

So if we apply the same technique to, say, a presentation of a new agricultural investment programme to a room full of pig farm directors, it will be obvious what details to focus on. They will be sending you a signal – "friend ?" But the earring in your left ear and your red hair dye will reply "foe!" "Friend?" he repeats with a faint trace of hope; "foe," says your Hawaiian tie, worn with a Gucci leather jacket. "Maybe possibly still a friend?!!" he pleads tearfully for the last time; "No, no, foe, fooooe!" shout back your cowboy hat and cigar. So, regardless of how persuasive your figures are and how strong the arguments, there is no chance your consulting company will be getting involved in the pig business!

- **Your pants.** OK, I know this is a Kama Sutra-esque book, but right now, I actually mean what's in your *pants pocket*? What is making all that rattling noise? Or is it something in the pockets of your jacket, perhaps? Pills in a plastic bottle, matches, keys? What is it that is making that jangling noise every time you move or take a step? These clanking objects have an amazing ability to distract the audience. And when your speech is long, these irritating noises have the maximum opportunity to annoy your audience. Maybe you also happen to have a habit of clicking your pen during the speech. I've witnessed several potentially good speeches go horribly wrong because of pen-clicking, although neither the audience nor the speaker realised at the time why it happened. So get rid of everything that makes a noise.

  Another thing is to take everything out of your pockets that might make your clothes stick out or bulge – glasses, a handkerchief, notepad, wallet, or a precious lucky charm. I know you might love your iPhone more than your own mother, but take it out as well. Take the pen out of your breast pocket – it might leak, and besides, that's where your handkerchief should go. Now I come to think of it, take the handkerchief out of that pocket too, unless you are a game show host.

Most importantly, remember to do all these things *before* you go on stage. When you are on stage and looking at the audience, you should no longer be buttoning your jacket, fixing your hair, shuffling papers or fixing your glasses.

I remind you again, dear readers, the success of any speech (and this has been proven on many occasions) is between 60 to 70% reliant on what the audience *sees*, 20 to 30% on *how* the speaker delivers their speech, and only 10% depends on *what* he is saying. So, please remember to be very thoughtful in what you wear before stepping onto the stage.

FAQ Chapter Six

1

Dear Radislav, I work at a company that sells software. We have quarterly seminar-presentations. And our problem is this: our software is demonstrated with a projector. For maximum visibility, the screen is moved as close as possible to the audience, the lights are dimmed, so the speaker has no other choice but to sit down in the front with his back to the audience. Basically, it's like sitting in a movie theatre – where the audience doesn't get to see the speaker at all, but only hear my voice coming to them from the dark. We can try using something more professional like Dolby Surround sound but it's a bit pricy, considering that our seminars are free. I would appreciate any advice you have on this. Thank you very much for your feedback, Alexander.

Firstly, it's not a good idea to completely turn the lights off – people should be able to write things down. Secondly, a presentation is a kind of advertising, which means that it is not the qualities of a product that are key, but the *image* of the product that is crucial. Consumers are likely to transpose the image of the presenter to the object that is being presented, not vice versa. My main point is that the audience needs to first fall in love with you, and only then should you shift their attraction and adoration towards the software that you are presenting. In other words, only 10 minutes into the presentation should you turn your computer on, dim the lights just a tad, maintain eye contact throughout, and demonstrate only the most crucial and impressive features of the software on the screen – and the rest of the time, put your face to work.

2

Dear Radislav, what do you do when there's no room for eye contact in your presentation? For instance, if the presentation consists of slides only and these slides are projected on to a wall. Only numbers and graphics get all the attention, and all you do in your speech is analyse what is shown on the slides. The audience does the comparison and analysis together with you, but there is no chance of establishing any eye contact. Ideally, I would like to stop doing these traditional presentations and set my own rules. Have you ever faced this problem? And, if so, could you please share your experience? Thank you, Anton.

I would advise you not to be too keen on "setting your own rules". Professionalism is all about reaching your goals while playing by the rule book in order to do so. Of course, if you were projecting slides on to a wall, it would be very difficult to make any eye contact. And what eye contact can we talk about if all the attention is all on numbers? Leave the listeners' eyes with your projector and take over their ears. You will have to work with your voice. More expressive pauses, questions that don't need an answer ("Don't you think?"; "Interesting, isn't it?"), shift the speed from time to time. You will only need eye contact at the beginning of the presentation, while the light is still on – and then again at the end.

Chapter Seven

They're All Ears...

This chapter explains how to capture and hold the audience's attention during your speech.

People very quickly forget approximately 90% of what they hear, 60% of what they see, and only 10% of what they do. This becomes very obvious when you think about it. What would you remember better? A story someone told you about how a person you don't know got into a fight? A situation where you witnessed a fight? Or a situation when it was you who got into a fight? The extent to which you are going to remember an event is determined by the intensity of your involvement in it.

A popular children's pantomime in Russia gives a great example of how involving people in an experience helps to make their learning go "deeper". In one scene, the scary, old witch, Baba-Yaga, asks the little kids in the audience: "Where did Ivanushka go? There?" – and the kids start screaming all at once and pointing in the other direction: "There! There !" Baba-Yaga, as if making a mistake, points in the direction he went: "That way?" The kids say (much louder and many of them jumping off their seats): "The other way!" This happens several times until the children in the audience are almost hysterical. The lesson they are learning here, of course, is that it's OK to lie to really evil people – and the "real-life", dynamic way they are learning it means the message will stay with them for a long time. This is a great illustration of the power of emotional involvement in making something stick in our memories.

Sadly, when people become adults, they stop using these engaging tools because they might seem childish. However, being a public speaker, you simply have to captivate your audience and, to do so, you might want to use one of the following tools:

- Ask the audience questions.
- As if inadvertently making a mistake, ask the audience to correct you.
- Ask those in the audience who have a post-graduate degree, subscribe to a business magazine, or play sports (depending on the topic of the speech) to raise their hands.
- Raise your own hand, starting a chain reaction and interaction between you and the audience.
- Ask people to move closer.
- Ask whether everybody can see the board and there are no flares, or if the lights need to be brighter, etc.
- Ask the audience if everyone has a copy of your speech's main points and, if not, ask the others to pass a copy to them.

These are all "distractors" and "ice-breakers" I made up myself as I went from public appearance to public appearance, and that means that you can do it too. The most important thing is to understand the principle of how it's done. I'm sure there are plenty of people out there who would describe these tricks as "childish". That may be so – but they work perfectly every time. Forget that the people in front of you are fully-grown adults wearing suits. Those serious frowns and business-like expressions are plastered on to make you think that they are important and serious people, when in fact, in many ways, deep down inside, they have remained the children they were at school. It may sound slightly disrespectful, but the second you start treating them as kids, they start behaving as if they were kids – and look up to you as if you were the only adult in the room. Often, when the audience is tired and I am the tenth speaker in a row that they are obliged to listen to, I say (with no irony): "Now kids, let's all look at me now. OK. Yes, right here. Look me in the eyes. Put your hands down and let's have some quiet." You'll be surprised, but this actually works – everyone is dead silent and looking straight at me. Childhood behaviour patterns can survive for a surprisingly long time, so public speakers can use that to their advantage, before getting stuck in to the serious part of their speech. As an example, early in his career, former French President Francois Mitterrand ran an ad campaign based on this exact principle. On all the election campaign leaflets and posters, he was photographed from a low angle. His hands extended in a welcoming gesture and his eyes were looking kindly into the camera. If you think about it, we have a similar version of that picture in our memories of when our dad used to come home from work:

He would come through the door, all tall and handsome, and stretch his arms out and scoop you up for a hug as you run to him. You'd breathe in his familiar day-old cologne, overlaying the smell of his workplace, and feel his stubbly cheek against yours. "Daddy's home!" you'd excitedly shout to your mother as a feeling of warmth and happiness settled into your mind.

This is exactly the feeling that Mitterrand's campaign tried to provoke in the French voters. Not through any direct instructions, but through a powerful and subtle image of security and love.

As well as the "taking the adult role" approach to engaging your audience, another way I have found to get them on your side actually involves putting yourself in an inferior position to them, by asking for help with something. It's very simple and you can come up with an almost infinite number of favours the audience can do for you. Sometimes, during my weekend training sessions, after I greet people on the first day, I'll ask them to help me sort out the chairs and place them in a circle. Notice though that I don't say, "Please do this now." I say, "Please *help* me do this," while pretending to have a backache. A couple of days into the training, I'll then reveal to them what I've been doing, and point out how many times it's worked – which really helps the effectiveness of this technique register with my trainees much better than just telling them would have done. To get your imagination going, here are a few things you can ask them to help you with:

- To keep an eye on the clock and let you know when 20 minutes is up

- To close the window
- To turn the lights off
- To distribute any handouts
- To call the people that are late
- To hush a neighbour in the audience

And even if it's only the one person who has actually helped you, everyone will feel like they've helped because the audience recognises itself as one organism.

One last thing to remember when engaging the audience is that you start with simple and easy tasks and slowly move on to more complicated requests, not the other way around. The same goes when asking them questions – if, from the start of your speech, you ask a question that needs a profound and deep answer, you'll find that the room goes silent. At the beginning, it's much better to ask questions that they can reply to with a nod: "Right?"; "Do you agree?"; "Shall I continue?" etc., so only later on will you be able to engage in a meaningful discussion with them and get very active feedback from your listeners.

FAQ Chapter Seven

1

Dear Radislav, I would like to ask if there is any way, with a psychological trick perhaps, that a speaker can get negative information across to listeners. Information that they don't want to hear and be overwhelmed with, but need to know for various reasons. Will their perception change if there is a change in tone of voice or speaking style? Looking forward to hearing from you, Olesia.

That's a very good question – it comes up a lot in emails. I have already mentioned that public speaking is, in a lot of ways, similar to seduction. Have you ever heard of a Don Juan going straight to the point? No, first, he creates an atmosphere – by telling the poor silly girl exactly what she wants to hear; all kinds of different things that are easily believable. And when he finally feels she is ready, when her heart is jumping out of her chest, her cheeks are flushed, and her breathing is deep and heavy, her movements jerky and hands are hot – this is when he tells her a scary and exhilarating truth... Imagine if he tried the same thing by saying: "Hey, baby, why waste time? You're attractive, so am I. The bushes smell like magic. Let's get to it!" He'd probably get slapped down by the girl and then beaten up by her boyfriend. The speaker needs to be smarter. If it really is the case that the audience does not want to hear about the information you're giving them, you have no other option but to smuggle it into the speech, after first grabbing their attention with your scintillating introduction.

This is why the speaker starts off by talking about the things the audience really cares about. To do that, you need to know who you are speaking to. If it's businessmen, then talk about opportunities to increase or save their capital. If it is women, then talk about opportunities to enhance and preserve their beauty, and so on; you can probably come up with openings accordingly. For one, kids are always a sure-fire hit – almost everybody has children or will someday have children. How do you then connect it to the topic of your speech? Easy.

You can use a trick I call "unbalance the audience". When someone is in a bored, dull state they can't really be reached and will usually default to having a negative response to what they're hearing – especially if it's information they are not going to like. To get through to them, you have to rock the balance and get them out of that state. To visualise this trick, I want to tell you a story about an immigrant taxi driver who got into trouble with the New York City Police for picking up a passenger on a street where he wasn't allowed to stop. The police officer that caught him wrote a report and, a few days later, the taxi driver had to appear before a judge. If found guilty, this incident could have had very unpleasant repercussions for the immigrant, including problems with potential citizenship and loss of job. The next day, he shared his problem (like taxi drivers in NY sometimes do) with one of his passengers, who turned out to be a communication specialist. The latter said, "Oh, you've really got yourself into trouble; American courts are a machine. Each one has a robotic judge who, after listening to the police report, asks you if you are guilty or not. If you say you are guilty, you get the minimum punishment. If you say you are not guilty, the case is revisited, but then, if in the process it then turns out that you are, in fact, guilty, you get the maximum sentence. There is a way out though – you can also say, "I am guilty with extenuating circumstances." If, in the revision of your case, none are found, you will, again, get the maximum sentence. But there are no other types of answers and all you need is to get the judge to listen to you. He listens to dozens of cases like that a day and just stamps them through on autopilot. You need to snap him out of that state, so that he will *see* you separately to all others." During the 40-minute journey, they came up with a plan. On the day of the court hearing, the cabbie came to the courthouse and stood in line, together with pimps, prostitutes, drug smugglers and traffic regulation offenders. When his turn came, he faced the judge. The police officer read the report. The judge turned to the cabbie and said, "Guilty or not guilty?" And the cabbie says, "*Not guilty* with extenuating circumstances!" The judge asked again and got the same answer. Then the judge leaned over his bench and asked if the cabbie's English was good enough to understand the question. He said that he thought his English was decent enough and asked the judge for the opportunity to explain what he meant. He was granted permission to do so. Then he recited the speech he had prepared: "Your honour, I want to bring your attention to one key detail – the place where this all happened. It happened on that God-forsaken 45th street. On this street, where dozens of pimps offer American citizens, women and girls for money; where drug-dealers peddle marijuana, cocaine and heroin; this police officer seemed to have noticed only one criminal – a poor taxi driver who picked up an honest American citizen who was standing there, soaking wet from the rain." The case was closed and the taxi drive got away scot-free.

What lesson does a good public speaker get out of this? Before trying to tell the audience something that they do not want to hear, shake them up. Tell them a story that will make them cry, suddenly yell something, or keep silent for 10 minutes. The Buddhists say that this is the time when the Anahata chakra (i.e. the heart chakra) opens up and you can place anything into it. This is a trick very well used in the advertising industry when commercials are aired in the middle of a captivating moment in a film.

The same trick works very well in everyday communication. Try it for yourself. It works like magic! I repeat: the trick is called "unbalance the audience".

2

Dear Radislav, up until recently, I have always made my presentations in languages that I speak freely, which is why I could effortlessly come up with examples, jokes or clever answers to questions. But now, I will need to host a two-day seminar in English. My level of English is above average, but I can still only read out the main points and briefly answer questions. I agree with you completely when you say that public speaking is comparable with sex, but what kind of a relationship can I build with the audience, when I'm afraid to even open my mouth? Thank you, Elena.

Dear Elena, yes, English isn't your mother tongue and you are struggling with it. Evidently, your audience speak the language much better. As you are very familiar with the comparison that the speaker is always in the position of a man and the audience is in the position of a woman –think what would a man do if his female partner was clearly better at making love than he is? Most men in this situation will try incredibly hard to portray themselves as modern Casanovas. If the woman is smart, the man's efforts will be laughable to her, although she will never reveal that to him.

In your situation, it is best to let the more experienced partner take over. This, however, does not mean you should not be participating – you should. One of the possible things to say would be: "You know, you are amazing at all the things that you do, darling. Why don't you continue doing what you're doing and I will be helping and learning as we go along, OK?"

In this situation, the man still remains a man, because he showed initiative in offering it gracefully to the woman.

How should this knowledge be used in public speaking? It is unreasonable to persuade your English-speaking listeners that you are the next Shakespeare, as the first word out of your mouth will prove otherwise. This is why you should admit up front that the audience knows the language better than you do, mainly because you have different backgrounds and ancestors. I have to warn you though that there is a world of difference between saying that you speak English worse than they do and saying that they speak better than you do. In the first case, you are submitting to the audience's superiority and appealing for their pity. In the second case, you are complimenting the audience, acknowledging their expertise and showing your respect for it. Admit this with a somewhat serious expression on your face and with a deep, slow voice. Take a pause after which, proudly raise your head, put a smile on your face and, in a higher-pitched voice, cheerfully proclaim, "That of course does not for a second mean that I am going to let you guys do all the talking here today – my English is definitely up to the job!" Obviously, this should be delivered with a strong sense of irony. At this point, you should see smiles on the faces of people in the audience. You can then begin your speech.

Another tip would be to allow your audience to guide you from time to time. For instance, suggest that they ask questions as you go, if something is unclear. They will not abuse that power, trust me. Don't forget to thank them for being so understanding, without being too sycophantic. I would also recommend that you memorise all the introductory and concluding phrases in English and rehearse them with suitable expressions and gestures.

3

Dear Radislav, what is "the intellectual level" of a crowd? Best, Andrey.

A room full of people need to have everything explained to them in great detail, whereas in a private conversation, a lot of the things you are trying to communicate can be made self-evident by the intimacy of your conversation. Your audience will get lost if you start using complex sentences; they will also have trouble with elaborate jokes. Generally speaking, the clowns falling over at a circus will always get more natural laughs than a complex and philosophical Woody Allen stand-up routine. So the simpler you keep your speech, the more people will understand and enjoy it.

4

Dear Radislav, let's suppose the speaker tells the audience an interesting story, maybe even a funny one – how would he then get them to concentrate again afterwards? Thank you, Denis.

If you try to go straight back to your presentation after a "funny story" diversion, you'll find that it's really difficult to get their attention, as although the subject has changed (from "fun" to the serious point you're trying to make), the focus of interaction hasn't. If you want to get their attention again, you need to quickly switch the focus to them by opening up the floor to a brief Q&A on what they've heard so far. They can even share stories that are similar to the general topic. This part, of course, doesn't have to last 20 minutes – you can make it much shorter. But when you do return to your topic, their attention will be completely focused on you. This always works. I often conduct training presentations up to eight hours' long, and the volume of material is so big that even a little attention leak by one of the participants could lead to big losses. Of course, this is not the only attention-holding technique I use, but it's the basic one. Without checking my watch, I know that a 20-minute attention cycle is coming to an end and it's time to switch the interaction style. My participants can tell you how this happens in theory, but in practice, they barely notice. They just feel that eight hours went by surprisingly quickly and admit that they didn't even doze off into a daydream, which often happens at much shorter lectures and seminars.

Chapter Eight

Duelling with
Your Audience

This chapter is for those who want to artfully reply to all questions that come their way, and come out of complicated situations on top.

A Q&A session after your presentation is a kind of game – but one that should have no winners, no losers or offended parties. But what do you do if you have the feeling that you are facing hostile questioning? Your first instinct would probably be to protect yourself and strike back. Unfortunately, if you have decided to become a successful public speaker, you'll need to deny yourself that pleasure. Try getting the same enjoyment from your Zen-like calm and stamina in withstanding attacks. But remember that it is much easier to actually keep your cool than to fake it when you are really raging. So try to stay focused.

The first and the most important thing: give up the misleading notion that you have to answer all the questions that come your way. You absolutely do not have to know everything in the world, or even everything in your professional area. You may also choose not to reply to a question because it's irrelevant, and not because you don't know the answer. Even if the reason for rejecting a question lies in your lack of knowledge or experience, honestly admitting this will have a much more positive effect on your reputation than attempts to cover it up with the illusion of absolute competence. People very quickly sense fake intentions. My purpose here is to show you how you can avoid answering a question without damaging the overall impression you are creating and wasting all the good work you've done up to that point.

Never say you don't *want* to answer a question. This would be very honest but I doubt that it's the kind of honesty that the audience would appreciate. It's better to say: "I'm sorry, I don't have any information about that at the moment..." or "I'd rather not give out any false information about that..." If the person insists on an answer, or if it is already the eighth time you've admitted that you don't have the information, use this old trick: write the question down and promise that you will get back to the person who asked it within the next 24 hours to let him know the answer. Ask him for his business card or write down his phone number. This looks professional and shows that you take the questions that you are asked seriously. Many of the presenters who use this trick almost never call back with an answer, but the audience will never find out about this, and you are left to make that ethical choice for yourself.

If you do find that you've made a mistake in some of the information you are giving your audience, or slipped up in the presentation of some facts or figures, don't try to hide it. By far the best thing to do is to admit your mistake and compliment the person who noticed it.

Dealing with "Intellectual Terrorists"

What do you do if someone disagrees with your point of view or questions the information you are presenting? Listen to this person carefully, while maintaining eye contact, and try to understand what the objection is. Make sure it's understandable (through facial expressions and gestures) to him/her and the audience that this point of view is very important to you. After you've let them get everything off their chest, begin your reply. Don't start out being rude or sarcastic, no matter how frustrating the "difficult customer" has been. So when you start, be cautious; never express embarrassment over tough questions or disagreements with somebody. I admit it's easier said than done, but this skill can be developed with special training. For now though, start your response with: "Thank you for this intriguing question," or "I see that I need to watch my step with you; happy to see someone so sharp in the audience", or "The problem you are describing is definitely one that deserves our attention", or something along those lines. After you've said that, talk about the subject, giving information you know or consider valuable to the listeners. Something like this: "But to really grasp this subject and answer your question, it is important to first understand this..." You have seen politicians and pop stars resort to this trick many times. They didn't come up with this trick all by themselves; they had professionals work with them. So you can do the same.

To be completely honest though, it often happens that the person asking these questions is not remotely interested in your answer. He is much more keen on sharing a bit of your limelight, trying to get attention by riding on your success and publicity. This is a kind of "intellectual terrorism" – and ultimately, it's all driven by the need for attention. Did you know that, in most cases, when terrorists take hostages, the first thing they demand is a TV – not a plane, not money, but a TV. Do you know why? Because they want to know that they are being talked about on TV. Maybe sometimes they aren't even aware of this need in themselves. In a similar way, the "terrorists" in your audience may sincerely think that they are raising their hand to get an answer. In reality, however, they just lack attention and want to get it in any way possible. They might have a feeling that they are not acknowledged or valued or noticed enough, so often, they would demonstrate their knowledge, sense of humour or courage when asking the question, rather than genuinely wanting an answer in good faith. The more we argue with them, the more agitated they will get and even a small amount of attention, positive or negative, will keep them going. So it's best to become their allies; point out to the rest of the audience how smart your interrogator is and how clever and intricate their question is. That may all sound impossibly patronising, but most of the spotlight-hunters will lap it up.

I once witnessed a famous Russian psychologist and head of a major training company speak at a conference, describing his training experience. When it was time for questions, a peculiarly-dressed girl raised her hand and said, "Have you no decency at all? We constantly listen to your lectures, we study psychology with the books that you've written, we idealise everything you say and do, and now you're telling us stories of how you're helping these Russian nouveau riche parasites rob our country!?" Talk about a friendly opening question, huh? But the psychologist didn't take long to reply. He's an extremely experienced professional and figured out quite quickly that everything about the way this girl was dressed and how she looked, and how the question was asked, pointed to the fact that she was one of those "intellectual terrorists". The best way to let such a person win would be to begin an open, public argument with her, but the speaker made a different move. He said, "What was your name again?" The girl replied "Dasha". Then he asked her where she went to school, which year she was in and what books of his she had read. He then invited her to stand up and said: "Why doesn't everyone take a good look at Dasha here. To be honest, looking at the modern generation of students, in the last couple of years, I've been losing faith in the future of psychology. But then I meet someone like Dasha – a sophomore psychology major – with her provocative question and obvious critical thinking skills and, you know what, my belief and hope in the new generation is restored once more. So thank you, Dasha, for that!" The audience erupted into applause, Dasha got what she wanted, the speaker got what he wanted, and the audience got what they were waiting for. The communications professionals in the room could only look on in admiration.

This, of course, is not the only trick in the book you can use against "intellectual terrorism". Simply ignoring them is still a highly-effective approach. Just like in that famous joke:

- *Doctor, Doctor, I am very upset and depressed, I feel like everybody is ignoring me.*
- *I see. Next?*

In this case, you assess the question or just thank the person for it and suggest another one. For instance, this is how Arnold Schwarzenegger dealt with a tricky question at his press conference in the midst of his election campaign for the Californian governor seat. A journalist asked, "Is it true that, when you were young, you did porn?" Aaaaw-kward... How do you reply? Do you admit to it and defend yourself by explaining how difficult it is for an immigrant to make it in the States without a dime? Do you joke about it and say that, yes, you did it and did it well? Do you deny it? Either way, it's a lose-lose situation. So what did Mr Schwarzenegger say? He said: "Oh, that's old news!" and gave the floor to the next reporter. This was very skilfully done, as he both answered it and didn't answer it at the same time, while doing it with consummate panache. Of course, he almost certainly has a team of speech-writers and image-makers, coaching him for these types of scenarios, but still you need to be quick on your feet. Try to learn from these two examples.

Something went wrong

If you suspect that you are going to be asked really unanswerable questions, you can resort to reverse psychology. For example, everyone knows that a sure-fire way to get beaten up by a street gang is to say, "Don't hit me!" to them. If you want a child to get scared and run away, you should sternly say, "Come over here right now!" For every action, there is an equal and opposite *re*action. So, when inviting the audience to ask questions, say something like this: "OK, it's time for questions now so please make them as tough as you can", or "I'll be happy to answer any questions you might have – but I do particularly enjoy the tricky ones." This way, you put everyone who wants to ask a question in a situation where you're proactively interacting with them, rather than passively reacting, because they are doing exactly what you're asking them to do. In my experience, an invitation like that will make anyone who wanted to start a dispute with you, rethink it. In fact, getting the audience on the back-foot like this will often result in them humbly asking if it's OK to ask "silly" or "easy" questions. Sometimes they even apologise for the question not being tricky enough: "My question may not be difficult but I would still like to ask it..." This usually amuses the audience, relives tension, and creates a perfect atmosphere for the end of your brilliant speech.

Extra strength

There are, however, situations in which, despite your knowledge and preparations, you end up face to face with a question that is so difficult or embarrassing that you're caught off-guard and backed into a corner. Perhaps this was the intention of the person asking the question, but what should your next steps be? If you try to fake your reaction or hide your feelings, the situation will get worse, so try not to do that. The best thing to do would be vocalise your feelings of embarrassment, but never say, "I'm humiliated" or, "I'm confused" – shift the responsibility onto the person asking the question by saying, "I must admit, *you made me feel* a bit confused" or, "Oh, I think *you've got me cornered* now"; "I have to say, you do *know how to debate, I'm way out of my depth on this one.*" Don't feel awkward about using these standard phrases. Catholics have the following aphorism about confessions: "If you blame yourself, God will absolve you; if you are making excuses for yourself, God will blame you." The same goes for the audience. At this point, an attentive reader will say – Wait a minute! Didn't the author already say that, under no circumstances, should the speaker go against and oppose the audience, because the audience sees itself as a whole organism, and by opposing one listener, you are thus confronting all of them? Yes, that is true, but there are exceptions. If you know for a fact that the member of the audience who asked the question does not represent the opinion of everyone in the room, let alone *your* opinion, then you can definitely take a stand against him, thus uniting with the rest of the audience. If you know that most of the room is on your side, with only a couple of opponents, then agreeing with them and trying to find common ground will only annoy the rest of your supporters, so attack if your position suggests so, and do it in a way that every ally in the audience would want you to. You will quickly become someone who said out loud what everyone else was thinking, and you'll see that from their approval. Today, you'll say things the audience is thinking, and tomorrow, the audience will be thinking what you are already saying.

Anxious person

Sometimes, you will get into situations where the person asking the question is extremely nervous, and the question comes out nonsensical and incoherent. In this situation, you can do one of the following things to help smooth it over:

1. Ask the person to repeat the question. Most likely, it will be much shorter and will make more sense the second time.
2. Repeat the question back to the person in the way you understood it and ask if that was what he/she meant.
3. Ask for a few minutes to think about it (meanwhile, keep answering other people's questions). During this time, you will either figure out what to say, or the audience will forget about the question.

Stick to one

What do you do if someone asks two, three or four questions at a time? That would be terribly hard because, at that moment, not only are you expected to reply in an honest, comprehensive and logical way, but also keep all of the four questions in your head at the same time. That is a difficult task, even for an experienced speaker, let alone a newbie. There is, however, something that can be done in advance to avoid this happening. Towards the end of your speech, you should make the point that, because of time limitations, you can only take one question per person:

"There is a large number of people who want to ask questions, but the time I have to answer all of them is limited, so I will have to insist that everyone only asks one question."

I once witnessed a chaotic storm of questions at a press conference that I organised for a very popular Russian rock musician and philosopher. It was one of my first ever events and I couldn't have predicted such a turnout before the event. A lot of people crammed into the room, and only a small proportion of them were actually journalists – most of them were adoring fans, each one trying to ask the star 10 questions at a time. Although the star held it together really well, it was a very intense experience, and didn't really work as a public engagement. It could have gone a lot, lot better if we'd stuck to the one question per person system.

Real difficulties

In some extreme situations, you may come up against an audience member who is difficult, not because they want to get in the spotlight, like our earlier example, but because they are simply a genuinely aggressive, unpleasant person who wants to make trouble for you by questioning everything you are saying. The best way to end this flow of unnecessary hostility is to kindly and patiently point out that the current format of this event doesn't allow for a discussion or exchange of opinions of any sort. Another quick way to put a stop to this is to say, "I'm sorry, I didn't hear the question" at the end of their tirade. Doing this once should get the message across to everyone else.

Question regimentation

The order in which questions are asked should be regulated by hand-raising. So try to keep this in mind because it will not look nice if a "rule-abiding" listener sits with his hand up in the air, waiting to be called on, and you answer questions that are being shouted out haphazardly by less civilised audience members. Respect the order that you yourself set, and ignore people who don't, otherwise the room will quickly fall into chaos that you won't be able to control. The same goes for the time allowed for each part of your speech – if you announced that you will be answering questions for 10 minutes, no matter how well you're doing, be strong enough to end your triumph on the turn of the 11th minute.

The silent treatment

It sometimes happens that there are no questions. At all. The speaker stands there smiling in dead silence. Embarrassing, isn't it? Typically, the speaker's nerves go, and after 10 seconds of waiting, he says with a sigh, "Well, if there are no questions, I'd better be going..." Now, let's be honest, that's not the most brilliant finale and, if you have done that in the past, I have to tell you: you were too quick to do so. Don't agonise about whether the silence was caused by the topic not being interesting enough – any topic can be made interesting if it's tied to events and situations that currently interest the audience. And don't fall into the trap of panic and self-recrimination. The key is to understand why silences like this often happen. Mainly, it's because it's difficult for someone in the audience to be the first to stand up and talk in front of everyone else. Much like it's always hard to be the first to start dancing at a club, but it's easy to be the twentieth to do so. So I suggest you give the audience a little nudge. Here are a couple of ways to do it:

- Give them a gentle push by saying the following with a genuine and encouraging smile: "OK, please go right ahead with the first question... yes?"
- If you notice even the slightest movement from a member of the audience, turn to him or her and see if there's a question there. Most likely, they are just hesitant about whether to ask now or later.
- Before your speech begins, ask someone you know (or maybe even someone you don't) to ask the first question to get the ball rolling. You may even want to get them to ask you a specific question.
- If the first way in this list didn't work, the second didn't happen, and you forgot to take care of the third one in advance, use this oldest trick in the book and ask yourself a prepared question by saying: "I am often asked such and such..." or, "Before I came on stage, I was asked an intriguing question about..." The minute you start answering, the flow of questions will start running. Just keep up with them.

Something to focus on while answering

An integral part of preparation for any public appearance is a prediction of possible questions and answers to them. For example, the US Presidential Administration has a special team of professionals that sum up all the information about the accredited journalists in Washington and, based on that information, come up with a prognosis of their possible questions before a press conference. What do you think is the percentage of questions they guess correctly? 80%! They guess more than half of the questions! So 80% of the questions have been prepared for and rehearsed; jokes, quotes, historical references have been written and worked through, speaker placement and gestures have been polished. If you've ever seen the American show, "*The West Wing*", then you'll know what I'm talking about. As a result of all this work, everyone sees the President as an even-tempered, smart and resourceful man. Do not give up on trying to make a similar impression, because answers to the audience's questions can completely change their perception of your overall performance. Here are a few points you ought to memorise:

- Never interrupt the person who's asking the question. Even if you have already grasped the gist of the person's thought, don't rush him to finish – wait until he or she is done talking. It is just plain rude. You might, if the person is taking up too much time, indicate with your facial impressions that it's time to wrap it up, you might even say "Right...", or "Uh-huh, and that means?" etc., but extremely politely, without offending anyone.

- The answer should never be as long as any part of your speech. Try to answer the question as briefly as you can. Ideally, every answer should be one phrase. Answers that are too lengthy kill the enthusiasm and put people off asking more questions.

- If the question has been asked quietly or unclearly, you should repeat it for the whole audience to hear. It is best if you always do that, because remember that the person standing is facing you and away from everyone else, thus maybe making it difficult for them to hear, so it's good if you always succinctly and quickly repeat the question for the whole room before answering.

- The most important thing is that you must not punish people for asking questions, and you cannot fail to engage with them. If you have been asked a question (regardless of its content), be sure to thank the questioner with at least a smile.

- When you answer a question, remember to keep your eyes on the person who asked it, because it is them you're replying to. When you answer it, make sure that the person is satisfied with the answer and your reply is sufficiently detailed. Beware of this overused go-to phrase though: "Did that answer your question?" Be more original, look for synonyms. Or maybe make eye contact with the listener and get some silent approval from him or her.

- A few small, encouraging comments on the questions you are being asked can be a very good way to ensure that they keep coming. Keep in mind, however, that the audience has zero tolerance for patronising lines like "That *is* a good question" or, "Wow – what an interesting question." Clichés like this will simply leave your audience feeling like you are a second-hand car salesman trying to manipulate them – so keep any comments you have as sincere as possible.

- Don't be afraid to evaluate questions critically either (without crossing the line into being rude or confrontational). Even a mildly critical response is better than no response at all. Keep in mind that the audience has a woman's mind. And there is nothing more irritating for a woman than indifference.

In summary, crossing swords with your audience can be one of the most intellectually rewarding parts of being a public speaker. The constant challenge to get the balance right between standing up for yourself and keeping them on side can be great fun – and mastering this aspect of the job gives you a very powerful tool.

FAQ Chapter Eight

1

Dear Radislav, I was giving a speech once, when the people at the back of the room started asking a whole bunch of useless questions and hogging my attention. How do I give enough attention to everybody without going overboard and allowing certain people to dominate? Thank you for your reply, Filip.

You can't let the audience have control of the floor until you want them to! Say: "Thanks for the input guys, but I'll be coming to your questions at the end of my presentation. Now let's move on..." Then immediately break off any eye contact with that part of the audience and move to a part where everything is calm. You can come back to the "cheeky" ones after a while, if you think that they have settled down and it's OK to do so.

2

Dear Radislav, my problem is with my vocabulary. I often get into situations where, speaking in front of an audience, I cannot find the right word quickly enough and end up saying a long "errrrr" instead. I then start the thought again, in the hope of remembering the missing word or term, but it comes out clunky and strange and everything just gets worse. Are there any exercises to avoid this problem? Thank you, Vaselisa.

Yes, there are actually several techniques to resolve the problem of forgetting a term or a word, or what you were going to say next.

- You can immediately skip to the next thought without even trying to remember what you have forgotten. While talking about the new topic, you might often find words that have slipped your mind before. If and when you remember them, I suggest you come back to it and say what you wanted to say.
- The second approach would be to begin formulating the same thought but using different words. However, if this does not work, move on to the next method.
- And finally, try holding on to the last couple of words of the last thought and building a thought from there.

This is how I do this exercise in my trainings. It's called "empty carriages". The task of the exercise is to keep talking non-stop for about two minutes; the meaning of the words is not important, what's important is the flow and coherency. Your voice and posture must show that you are saying things that make perfect sense, while you might be saying complete nonsense. Usually, the group suggests the first line. Let's say it's "Birds migrate to warm countries". Your speech may sound something like this: "Birds migrate to warm countries in the winter. Which warm countries? Must be the countries that have warmer weather while it's cold here. Why is it cold here? Because it's the winter. Winter, as you know, is different from summer in the sense that, this time of year, the temperature goes down. Temperature is measured in Celsius degrees. I don't know who Celsius is but I am familiar with the word 'degree.' For instance, 40 degrees does not necessarily have to be a measure of temperature, it could also be the strength of an alcoholic beverage. And, whenever I speak of strength, I remember how I saw a man pull a monster truck by a rope..." etc. What this exercise does is to develop your skill of coming up with the right word quickly, and also takes away the fear of stumbling. As a result, you make less mistakes in real situations. I recommend that you start with two minutes of this exercise a day. You can then gradually increase this to 10 minutes. Write back to me in a month and tell me if there was any progress with your problem. Good luck!

3

Dear Radislav, once, after hearing me answer all his questions, my opponent said that "answering questions straight away without giving them any thought is a sign of poor taste". I would like to hear your professional opinion on this matter. Thank you, Tatiana.

Tatiana, I hate to admit it but your opponent is right. Giving questions a few seconds of thought is a sign of respect for the person asking the question. You might want to think through the question first so that you can present them with the best and most profound reply you can. You want to choose your words carefully. Secondly, the person who asked the question will have an ego boost, thinking that he has cornered you. If you want to enhance this effect further, begin your answer by acknowledging the unusualness of the question and its uniqueness: "You sure asked a tough one this time!" or, "What an interesting question", and so on. The main secret here is that, during your speech, you should try to direct your attention towards the audience. If you answer with no hesitation, without giving the questions any thought, it might appear unprofessional. Your ultimate concern, while on stage, is the audience's feelings and thoughts, not your personal glory. Imagine a dentist who's captivated by his own skill, or a masseuse who can't look away from his biceps. My point is, when answering questions, don't be afraid to look silly – the audience adore that. This means if you are asked a question, do not be afraid to look like an idiot. The audience will love it.

4

Dear Radislav, a lot of the times during my company speeches, questions that come up are usually addressed to my boss and not to me. I still try to answer them because I usually know more about the subject than my boss does. My boss is OK with it, which is good. But I'm worried that he'll think I have ideas above my station. What do you think? Thank you, Nikolay.

Well, it seems like your boss has no sick pride to deal with and is very flexible. If you actually want to outdo him then go for it! The King is made by his court. If the footman steals all the attention, the King will lose his position very quickly. If your career and inner peace are important to you, try acting illogically. If you hear a question that you have a good answer to, find a way to delicately pass it on to your chief, explaining this by his high competence in this issue. If you will be doing this regularly, he will start doing the same thing to you. Otherwise, you might get totally pushed out of the presentation and out of your job. Remember that the power of action is equal to the power of counteraction.

5

Dear Radislav, what should I do in a situation where there is a person in the audience that I'm not in a very good relationship with. The sort of guy that is always trying to get me into trouble. I can't ignore him completely, but if I start giving him all of my attention, I will lose the audience, and if I try shutting him up, that will disturb me and I will lose my train of thought. Ideally, I would like to ask him to leave the group but that might just turn into more trouble. What would be the best way of handling this? Let me know, thank you, Oxana.

The audience recognises itself as a unified organism. The speaker in this case is an alien to them. At least at first. You should try to never get into any kind of conflict with the audience but rather interact with them, because if you begin to bully or pick on a member of the audience, then they will defend him as "their guy". I would not advise you to do that.

It doesn't necessarily mean that, if you give someone apparent attention, you will immediately "lose the audience". If while answering this person's question, you maintain eye contact with the rest of the room, nothing bad will happen. Just to be absolutely safe though, try establishing some sort of order of your presentation; for instance, that the questions will only be answered at the end and only by raised hands. I don't remember a single case when the audience refused this. If this person continues to make remarks during your presentation, you can remind him of the order, which was agreed on by the whole group. If he violates the order still, he has then opposed himself to the audience as a whole, not you personally, and that's a different story.

Depending on how rude and annoying he is, you can either ignore him while you are answering questions from others or decide with everyone that questions will be taken in writing. Although, I have to say that a lot of the time, in reality, it turns out that usually these "bad" people are not as bad as you think they are.

CHAPTER NINE

Testing, One, Two, Three...

This chapter explains how to work that microphone.

A street vendor is selling bananas on a crowded street in Paris. From time to time, you can hear people asking him how much he charges for one. "Twenty sous, Mademoiselle." "Twenty sous, Mademoiselle." "Twenty sous, Mademoiselle," he answers each time. But the next time he hears the same question, he responds: "Twenty sous, Madame." "Excuse me," protests the woman, "why did you call everybody else a Mademoiselle and referred to me as 'Madame'?" "Well," the vendor replies, "it's just the way you grabbed it, Madame..."

Get a hold of it

Let's start with the simplest task – holding the microphone. How does one hold it without giving away that this is your first time speaking publicly? The key is to hold the microphone the way you'd hold a fork, and not the banana from the joke above. Use the tips of your fingers only – don't try to grab and squeeze it with your whole hand. At the same time, make sure that all your fingertips are resting on it and that your little finger isn't sticking out as if you're sipping tea from a delicate porcelain cup. Your elbow should be relaxed and lowered so that it's resting gently against the side of your ribs. A typical mistake here would be to raise your elbow as high as your chin, which would make you look like a bugler at an army camp.

You should keep the microphone at the same distance from your mouth throughout the whole speech. To determine the optimum placement for the microphone, bring a closed palm up to your mouth so that your index finger is touching your lips. So wherever your ring finger is at that point is where the mic is supposed to be. If you keep it further away, your voice will not be as nice to listen to; if you keep it closer to your mouth, your "p" sound will make an unpleasant noise, so try to keep that distance from the start to the finish of your speech.

The microphone needs to mirror all your movements. When you lean forward, tilt the microphone forward as well, when you turn, the mic turns with you. As you know, earthlings see the same picture of the moon's surface because it always revolves around the Earth with the same side turned towards it. This means that, no matter where you point the camera at the moon, you always see the same face. You must symbolically mirror this natural phenomenon while speaking with a microphone: wherever you turn, the microphone should turn with you.

Your movements are naturally a little constrained when you're speaking into a microphone. I usually recommend that if you're left-handed, you should hold it with your stronger left hand (and vice versa if you're right-handed), leaving your "weaker" hand free to gesticulate and enhance your point when needed. It's important to remember though that as you are using your "weaker" hand to gesticulate, you may have a tendency to make smaller, less visible gestures. Try to compensate for this by exaggerating them slightly. Most importantly, the one thing that you should *never* attempt to do is to gesticulate with the hand that's holding the microphone. This is a classic mistake for people who are new to the art of speaking publicly, and can get hugely irritating for the audience, because of the constant change of the sound level as the mic moves to and from your mouth. If you've ever seen a public speaker do this, you'll know how annoying it can be.

Technical stuff and how to work the mic

Make sure you check the location of the speaker system before your speech, be especially cautious if the speakers are behind you, and remember that if the microphone gets too close to them, the feedback will cause an ear-splitting screech that will have the audience wincing with their fists pressed over their ears, and the sound engineer muttering less than complimentary things about you under his breath. If and when this happens, the main thing to do is not to panic, and don't get upset; just quickly turn the microphone away from the speakers and continue talking.

If you're using a microphone with a cord, then let the hand that's not holding the microphone get the cord out of your way as you move around on stage. With time and experience, this will become an instinctive action.

Many professional performers do this so gracefully that it underlines their confidence and professionalism, increasing their reputation as a great public speaker. An inexperienced speaker who steps on the cord can look rather comical when, in the midst of a complex speech, a very expensive microphone suddenly jumps out of their hands like a wild rabbit. Or if the cord suddenly gets unplugged and the whole of the audience is treated to the peculiar sight of the sweating speaker desperately trying to shove the cord back into the damn microphone! The best outcome of all, of course, is to have one of the more modern, cordless microphones, or even one of those snazzy headset mics. Having said that, there is a slight drawback, even with these newer types of microphone, in that due to the fact that there's much less "white noise" produced by them, it can sometimes be difficult to tell if they're actually switched on or not. An inexperienced speaker will always give himself away when he taps on the mic to see if it's on, or when he sheepishly tries the whole "One-two, one-two..." routine. I would suggest to just get started straight into your speech – the audience's reaction will quickly tell you if you are being heard or not. And one more thing – before all of the above issues can be taken care of, make sure you have learned how to actually switch the microphone on in the first place.

Now, about the microphone stands. There are two types of microphone stands: telescopic stands and boom stands – the difference is obvious. Your typical telescopic stand is more difficult to work with for two reasons: one is that, if you have a bit of a belly, you won't be able to bring the microphone close enough to get the best sound out of it. The second reason is that telescopic stands are much more difficult to adjust to your height. A typical mistake that a lot of first-time speakers make is talking into a microphone that's set at the height that the previous speaker used. As a result of this mistake, you can be treated to such amusing sights as a tall CEO standing hunched over the with their eyes facing the floor, as if they were addressing a small child. Or a short speaker with their head straining so hard to reach the microphone that all the audience sees for the entirety of their speech is the speaker's neck. So, if you will be using a telescopic mic stand, please make sure you get used to it prior to coming up on stage, and practise adjusting it to your height.

Boom microphones, on the other hand adjust easily, so there should be no problem there, although, there are two things to keep in mind with them as well. Firstly, when you adjust the stand, it will make a squeaky sound that is amplified via the microphone. To avoid that, turn the mic off when adjusting it and then back on again. Usually, all modern microphones have a *mute* button on them so use that, without anyone even noticing (try not to use the on/off button, because that will be much more noticeable). Secondly, when you adjust the stand according to your height, note that the angle of the boom changes as well, so be sure to keep it parallel to the ground with a slight tilt forward. It might also happen that, during the speech, you will be overcome with such great excitement that you will grab the mic off the stand and begin to pace around holding it. That is always a good thing, but keep in mind that when you take the mic off the stand, it might also produce an unpleasant squeaky noise, so use the *mute* button here again. Also, the stand that you will no longer be using will need to gracefully be set to the side of the stage – please don't leave it in the centre.

If you're given a headset mic, it will definitely free your hands and overall movement, as you will no longer be "tied" to one place or using just one hand, but there is one thing to be aware of when using a headset. The off/mute button will most probably be located on the transmitter that in turn will be attached, either to the back of your trousers or skirt, or to the headset itself. Either way, it will not be easy to reach and switch off and, as a result, it will amplify literally every sound you make, so keep in mind that if you burp, cough or sneeze, it will be heard by everyone in crystal-clear surround sound.

Sometimes there are situations when the speaker is sitting down at a desk with the mic in front of him or her. Those types of microphones are usually especially sensitive and sound engineers set them up to work based on a specific distance the sitter will be from the mic. This means that, when you are speaking, you should try not to lean into the mic too much, even if you feel that your voice sounds much quieter – that is normal. If the audience, for whatever reason, can't hear you, they will notify you very quickly, so don't strain your voice, and keep away from the microphone at the distance I have already mentioned.

If you are being interviewed, the person asking the questions will normally hold the microphone for you. Resist the temptation to fight for control over the mic; remember that the journalist is a professional and knows where to hold it in order to get the perfect sound. Do not worry, the mic will keep up with you no matter where you turn or move.

There is also such a thing as a clip-on microphone, which, as the name implies, attaches to your clothes with a clip. Once it's on, you don't need to worry about it at all because it's not going to move from where you've clipped it. Having said that, if you are being interviewed live on air, try to make as few movements as possible, as they tend to pick up every sound your clothes make on your skin. High-quality microphones don't have this problem, but the cheapest one can cost up to $500 , so the chances of working with a good one are slim.

An important point to keep in mind

Here's something that I would like to plant in your mind. I appreciate the unlikelihood of you having picked up this book as someone who's already fully able to skilfully and flawlessly use a microphone on stage. So, if you want to turn the knowledge gained here into a skill, you need to practise. Start by finding an object that resembles a microphone in your house – I recommend you use a banana because it's similar in both size and weight. Tie a cord to it and rehearse your speech with movement and gestures. While doing this, make sure to move the cord from under your feet so you don't trip over it. Don't forget to maintain imaginary eye contact with the audience, and after you're done... eat the banana.

After your banana rehearsal, I would suggest you get to the venue of your real presentation in advance; walk around the stage, make yourself acquainted with the surroundings, ask the sound engineers to switch the microphone on (and show you where the mute button is), try lifting the stand to feel its weight and get used to it, practise adjusting the stand according to your height, etc. etc. Talk into the microphone and get used to the sound of your own voice and the volume at which it's coming out of the speakers. All this will make you feel much more relaxed and confident.

And one last thing to remember is that most of the people giving speeches for the first time don't know a quarter of what you now know. So now's the time for training and practise – get to it !

FAQ Chapter Nine

1

Dear Radislav, I recently started teaching at a university, and after reading your recommendations, the contact with my audience very much improved. But I have another question in regards to the use of the microphone: what do I do with it? I only know of one rule, which is that it needs to be switched from one hand to the other from time to time. How else do you recommend I manipulate it to feel comfortable while speaking? Thank you, Marina.

Try juggling three microphones while bending forward on one leg – that really helps you to feel comfortable. No, but seriously, comfort is not something that comes from manipulating a microphone and it's best not to play around with it too much, but to keep it at a set distance from your mouth throughout your speech. Try to avoid abrupt exhaling, or if you need to cough or, God forbid, hiccup, take the microphone away from your mouth – otherwise, the audience will hear an unpleasant sound very loudly. It makes sense to rehearse with the microphone that you will be working with because different types have different nuances and you need to know your tools before you go on stage. And make sure that the organisers give you a microphone for speaking – there are ones that are made precisely for singing and these are no good to speakers because the sound quality is different.

2

Dear Radislav, is there a difference in how your voice sounds with and without a microphone? Thanks, Peter.

Microphones slightly distort your voice, but a good mic, together with finely-tuned equipment, make the voice fuller and deeper. You should speak in the same way you speak in real-life, but remember not to get too close to the speakers because you'll hear a very loud, nasty sound.

3

Dear Radislav, is it better to speak loudly or quietly during a speech and in general? There's a theory that speaking quietly makes the audience listen more attentively and actually hear what the speaker is saying. Do you think that's true? Dmitry.

Yes, Dmitry, it's a common opinion that if you speak quietly, the audience needs to concentrate in order to hear you. And unless you're talking complete nonsense, they won't drift away again. The very best way to guarantee attention though is to vary your delivery throughout your presentation. Try switching your voice from quiet to loud and back again, try walking around then stopping, try making bigger than usual gestures, and so on. You need to keep the audience interested. If you just stand still on stage and speak quietly, it might work for a short period of time, but then it will annoy the audience and their attention will be lost.

CHAPTER TEN

Important tips

This chapter is a collection of small but important tips on public speaking that can make a good speech into a great one.

The tighter the better

If you want to successfully manage your audience's emotions, keep in mind that an audience scattered across a big room is much less perceptive. Experts say that emotions are contagious, thus, people sitting closer together in the audience laugh much harder at a joke than separate individuals, seats apart. This is what's known as emotional infection. But the trick here is that this syndrome only works when people are sitting (or standing) close to one another. The same goes for righteous indignation, or any other feelings you want to arouse in your audience.

So when you are researching a venue for your speech, pick one that will ensure that everybody sits close to one another. This is why a smaller space that is filled to capacity is much better than a big one that is only half-full. If you have no say in this then use a trick that I have used myself many times. If I had to speak in front of 200 people in a room for 600, I would extend a string between the 10th and the 11th rows, so the listeners had no choice but to fill the first 10 rows with 20 seats in each one. If string is not an option, you may want to put a note on the seats for people not to sit there, or block the entrance off with a chair or a microphone stand, or with anything you can think of. It's very important to block those rows off. If, for whatever reason, all of the above is impossible, in the first couple of minutes on stage, the speaker can politely ask the listeners to move forward. It's most likely that no one will move at first. Be polite but persistent – once the first person budges, the others will follow – it's the herd instinct and it will eventually prevail. It's been proven. You will have a much easier time on stage if you do this beforehand. A popular Soviet and post-Soviet pop singer, Valeriy Leontyev, once said that one empty seat in a room drew a lot more energy out of him than a hundred seats filled with people. In addition to all the above, there is another positive effect in sitting people closer together – empty chairs in the auditorium are just as off-putting for the audience as they are for the speaker. The people who have come may feel as if they have come to listen to something others seem to have no interest in – so if you can get rid of those chairs, you can at least create the illusion of a full house. Participating at a sold-out show is much more flattering and enjoyable for everyone who's come to it than being somewhere no one else bothered to turn up.

Tempo

Many amateur speakers, especially the ones who come on stage for the first time, tend to speak much too quickly. It is important to remember that the subjective perception of time for the speaker, and for the audience, are different, meaning time moves at different speeds for you as it does for them. Because of the adrenalin flow in your body, which makes all the natural processes in it work faster, it might seem to you that you are speaking at a normal speed, when in fact, you are rattling on uncomfortably fast. Seeing you speak like that, the audience will feel that you're rushing through your speech and will register that as a lack of confidence. You might *think* that you're speaking slowly enough for everyone to follow, but the audience can hardly keep up with what you're saying. You might *think* that it's time to move to the next subject, but the audience hasn't yet understood what you said in the previous one, and so on. So I would urge you to try to speak slower, and to remind yourself to slow down every once in a while. If you are notorious for rushing through your speech, use unusual methods to remind yourself not to. For example, a student of mine would put a sticker on the inside of the podium from which she was speaking that said "Slow down!"

I would also suggest doing the following: an hour before going on stage, slow down everything you're doing and deliberately exaggerate the slowness of all your actions. Talk, walk, move, answer the phone slowly and, as a result, your inner timing will slow its tempo, making it easier for you to speak and enunciate everything evenly on stage. Although it may sound a bit silly, this exercise really helps, I promise.

However, it's important to remember that, to retain the audience's attention, just slowing down your tempo is not enough. As I have mentioned before, to keep them on their toes, you have to maintain contrast and variety in your speech. As long as the basic tempo of your presentation is comfortable for your audience, then you can try to experiment with occasional changes in speed, as long as they add to the expressiveness of your presentation. Introducing occasional bursts of higher tempo, followed by carefully chosen pauses and returns to the slower speed, can create very powerful communicative effects in what you're saying.

You – your – yours

I have read many times that a person loves to hear the sound of their own name and likes the way it sounds. Sales and negotiations professionals are advised to address their colleagues by name. Of course, a speaker standing in front of 200 people can't address them by name, but it is important that you find a friendly, informal way to refer to the collective group of people who have gathered to listen to you. The key thing to bear in mind is that people that are present in a room should always be referred to in the second person, not the third. So the following ways of addressing your audience are basically unacceptable:

"I would like to thank those who are present here today..."

or

*"I would like to let those present here today
know..."*

This use of the third person can't help but make your
audience feel like you are addressing someone other
than them, so stick to phrases like:

"I would like to thank all of you..."

or

"Thank you all for joining me today."

To illustrate the power of the second person address
even more clearly, imagine if all amorous men said:

"I love the girl who is present here right now."

instead of

"I love you."

I think the difference is pretty clear. The same basic
idea applies to a famous Russian toast, which is always:

"Let's drink to you, dear ladies."

and never

"Let's drink to the ladies of this house."

How long to stay at it

In his novel, "*The Possessed*", a great Russian writer and thinker, Fyodor Dostoevsky, pointed out:

> "*How can anyone expect to keep an audience like ours listening for a whole hour to a single paper? I have observed, in fact, that however big a genius a man may be, he can't, with impunity, monopolize the attention of an audience at a frivolous literary reading for more than 20 minutes.*"

Dostoevsky was, of course, talking about a light and easy literature reading, but with more serious topics, it's even harder to keep the audience's attention, so limit your triumph to twenty minutes, which is approximately six pages of text.

Ron Hoff wrote a book called "*Say It In Six*", where he convinces us to shrink any presentation down to six minutes. He gives perfect examples of how brilliant speeches can fit into 360 seconds, and it is truly fascinating. But I tend to agree with Dostoevsky: 20 minutes is a maximum because 20 minutes is how long the attention span of a human being is. A class at school lasts 45 minutes: 20 minutes to settle down and repeat new material, and 20 minutes to learn the new chapter. The same thing goes for grown-ups. If, for any reason (volume of information, traditions, length of the speech), the speaker cannot limit his speech to 20 minutes, he'll need to change the activity: after listening for 20 minutes, have them ask questions, then show slides, then a video, then go back to the speech. If the speech is very lengthy, try splitting it into parts with breaks in between. Even short ones. This will allow you to deal with a renewed attention span every time.

Remember that, while listening to a speech, people cannot go back to the beginning, as they would in a book, so do not be afraid to repeat and sum up certain parts. The same goes for the end of your speech – you should remember to warn your audience in advance: "Before we move on to the questions..." or "In conclusion..." etc. Try to avoid using the popular phrase, "And one last thing...", which gets repeated over and over again, thus killing the audience's hope that they have finally made it to the end of the speech.

Why "old" Lennox Lewis beat the speedy David Tua

Professional boxing fans are sure to remember the fight between Lennox Lewis and David Tua. For those of you who aren't boxing fans, the key point is that Lewis was 36 years old – practically ancient for this sport, and at 27, Tua was still just coming into his prime. What's more, in the run-up to this fight, Tua had beaten a number of other contenders for Lewis' title in pretty swift and brutal fashion, and was obviously very hungry to dispatch the old-timer and make the title his own. In the event, though, although Tua came out fast and furious for the knockout from the first round, it was actually the much more passive and laconic Lewis who was given the fight, on the judges' decision, in the 12th round. Tua was the hungrier, more aggressive fighter – but all of his sound and fury played into the hands of the careful, technical skill of Lewis – and it was this "management" of the fight that impressed the judges and gave Lewis the victory. What does this have to do with public speaking? Basically, the point I'm trying to make here is that, although passion and conviction are important, don't overdo it and try to hammer your audience into submission with the points you are making. If they feel like you are furiously trying to convince them of something, they will start to resist – so don't let them see how keen you are to win their approval. Show a laid-back, healthy amount of indifference and you will win the fight with the subtlety of Lennox Lewis.

How to choose the location for your performance

This is an issue that usually gets neglected, but which may substantially influence not only how you feel, but whether your speech is successful. Firstly, the choice of location from which you will speak may be determined by what has happened there before you. For instance, if the speaker before you was lousy and bored the audience, try to stand as far away from where he stood as possible. Don't go overboard – try not to make that spot too remote, but definitely avoid spending much time in it. If the person before you was one who has read this book, you can be sure that his performance was so impeccable that the audience didn't want to let him go, so stand in his exact place. Your job now is to outdo him.

Make sure that there are no open doors, windows and spaces behind you. This will keep your survival instinct at bay, which will otherwise leave you with the slightly anxious feeling that someone could attack you from behind. Close the door and close the curtains if there are windows. It is also extremely difficult to give a speech with a presidium (people sitting at a desk behind you). Again, your self-preservation instinct might not be as trusting as your conscious mind, and you may find yourself feeling twitchy about having the people in the presidium behind you, out of sight. The uncomfortable feeling of someone watching you from the back can throw you off course and add to your anxiety. Try to find a place to stand to the side of the table, so that you can see the people at the desk with your peripheral vision. Again, these may sound like tiny details, but trust me; they can make a serious difference.

What to stress

In my trainings, I often have to frequently reiterate the fact that speakers tend to underestimate the importance of the emotional component while talking to their listeners. Working with the audience is not a meeting of minds, but rather a meeting of hearts; yet we keep stressing facts, numbers and arguments. If facts and arguments were enough to persuade somebody to do something, there would have been no such thing as advertising and marketing; there would only be lists of the products' qualities. In fact, that's what advertisements used to look like in the old days. Most of this book is based on the idea that public speaking is more about seduction than logical argumentation. It is hard to seduce someone with facts, isn't it? Knowing this, some speakers go too far the other way – turning a speech into a show, with jokes and entertainment. Whether that's a good way to go is a different question and depends on *when* your listeners are expected to make a decision. Here is how this can be determined, but first, let's look at how a person makes a decision, any decision. It is commonly accepted that both spheres of the human brain carry out different functions simultaneously. The right one operates with images, feelings, emotions – consequently, it is responsible for the arts, aesthetics, fantasies and, in general, the humanities. The left one is responsible for exact sciences, arguments, facts and rationalisation.

The moment you are making a decision (and that happens practically non-stop – do I smoke now or later, do I open the door with this hand or the other, do I hold the door open for the girl in front of me, do I flip through TV channels, do I stand in this traffic jam or do I try to go around via a side street? – the work of our brain is distributed between hemispheres unequally. The right hemisphere (the irrational, the emotional) takes up 80% in the decision-making process, while the left hemisphere is tasked with the remaining 20% of involvement. Post the decision-making process, the brain begins rationalising the choice we just made, and the workload is redistributed in the exact opposite proportion. The person is trying to figure out if he has made a mistake or not. Of course, no one likes to think they've made a mistake, hence the constant attempts we all make at rationalising our decision as the right one.

So there you have it: if your audience is supposed to be making a decision directly as a result of your presentation, I would advise you to *stress the emotional component*. If your audience will be making their decision after further careful consideration, then do the opposite – *stress the figures, facts and rational arguments*.

For instance, a typical mistake politicians make during an election campaign is to rely exclusively on whipping up support through the use of inspiring speeches and powerful imagery that connects straight to the emotions of the people in the room, forgetting that, by the time these people come to vote, they may actually have reflected on the content of what the politician was saying and found it to be empty. That's why you need to have a flexible approach, as mentioned above – rely on the fact that it is a right-brain emotion that communicates when you're dealing with people in the room, but never underestimate the need to give them some actual content that will still seem valid, interesting and relevant when they are doing their left-brain reflecting on it later.

St Sebastian

I love public speaking because you can use different tools to reach the same result. The downside, of course, would be that sometimes, using different tools can also lead to unexpected results.

Here's a story I would like to share with you. I got my first degree at university, majoring in linguistics. Like most of my classmates, I had no plans to work as a schoolteacher, given the pretty horrible working conditions this job entails in Russia. I was preparing myself for work in the world of science, and by the time

I graduated, I had already had several papers published, spoken at a few conferences, and had chosen the topic of my PhD dissertation. But life had a different plan for me. My high school teacher of Russian and Literature, who still worked at my old school, asked me if I could substitute for him with one of his classes for a term. He was trying to enrol in a seminary, but the headmaster would not let him go, seeing as there was a constant shortage of teachers in Russia at the time, especially male teachers. At first, I was quite reluctant, but this teacher had been a great influence on me, so I felt I should return the favour. Despite my reservations, in the end, I ended up staying at the school much longer than was originally intended. I wasn't consciously aware of it at the time, but what attracted me to teaching was that it was a perfect opportunity to practise public speaking. On average, a teacher has five classes a day, with very different and incredibly demanding audiences every time. Sincerity is the only thing that unites all of them – children are painfully honest in their instinctive reactions. If they do not like your lesson, they won't try to fake it out of politeness by looking at you and pretending they are listening carefully (unless, of course, the teacher has successfully terrified them into doing so). If you don't quickly develop the ability to hold their attention, you will spend most of your day struggling to refocus absent gazes, and drown out background whispering and shuffling. However, if you have the twin bonus of something interesting to say, and an engaging and inspiring delivery, you'll experience the teacher's dream of rapt silence and all eyes on you. When it's successful like this, teaching can be an addictive job, despite all the hassles that go with it.

To round off this little trip down memory lane into my teaching past, I would like to share one of the best classroom management techniques I picked up from this time of my life, which I have found equally as useful in the grown-up world of public speaking to adults. This technique is one you should keep in your toolbox for really drastic situations, when you just can't get the audience's attention. For example, I used to use it with classes who had just come back from PE and were still running on adrenaline, or for those difficult classes at the end of the term when their minds are already on holiday, but you still need to cover a lot of ground with them. I call the trick "St Sebastian", after the famous religious painting of the saint, shot full of arrows, with a sorrowful but accepting look on his face. Here's how it worked for me in class:

If the class were really out of control and there was no chance of getting their attention, I would come in, take my place in the usual spot in front of the class, lower my arms to my side and then freeze. My gaze would be directed at one spot above the children's heads, and I would stay fixed on that spot, no matter what. There would be no reprimand or reproach in my eyes; everything about them should say, "Forgive them, Father, for they know not what they do", just like St Sebastian as the arrows hit home.

What would happen next? Nothing, at first. Very soon after that, a few students who cared about my opinion would demonstratively sit upright and be quiet. Then they would signal the other kids to be quiet as well, meaning that nobody would be left with the excuse that they hadn't seen the teacher. After a while, as the silence grew around the increasing minority of noisy pupils, they would one by one join the silent majority under the pressure of the situation. Once I finally had the complete silence and attention I was looking for, I would remain silent myself for a few more seconds, then lower my gaze, establish eye contact with the listeners and, without a shade of reproach, say hello and begin the lesson.

To be completely honest, the first time I tried this, I did not think it would work. I had always assumed the typical methods of rhythmically banging a pen against a table or shaking a book in the air and shouting, "Silence!!!" were the best ways to get what I wanted. But as I'd learned from experience, often, this extra noise would just add further impetus to the noisy pupils to make more of their own. It was the repeated failure of the "make a louder noise yourself" approach that led me to try out St Sebastian.

When I finally decided to use it, I thought it would take a while. I even timed it. I entered the classroom and did everything as above. I stood and I stood. And I kept thinking to myself: "Am I just going to be standing here like an idiot for the whole lesson? How long have I been doing this already?" – but, eventually, miraculously, it worked – and when I looked at my watch, I saw that it had only actually been two minutes!

After using this technique a few times, I noticed that it could be used, not only for getting attention and quiet at the start of a lesson, but also for regaining attention if it had been lost during the lesson. All I needed to do was freeze for a second with the St Sebastian look and all eyes would again be on me. It was my way of emphasising again and again that "I only speak when I am listened to".

As childish as it may seem, I have found this technique to be absolutely transferable to the world of presenting to adults. I just want to remind you again that it should only be used as a drastic measure, when your audience is tired, drunk, have just returned from a big lunch, or are otherwise not particularly focused on what you're saying.

Breathing

A professional speaker takes very little air into his lungs, and does so in short breaths. And he doesn't breathe in again until all the air is exhaled. A beginner takes in several cubic metres of air, and attempts to make his whole speech while exhaling them. Not having fully exhaled, he will then take another breath, expanding his ribcage to the max. What happens when he does that? If you remember your school science lessons, the air on our planet contains five times more oxygen than the human body needs. As a result, the speaker is oversaturated with oxygen, which leads to oxidation, which leads to dizziness, then to intense heartbeat, then to redness in the face, sweating, confusion of thoughts, embarrassment, panic, hysteria, ambulance, ER, IV. None of which makes for a good presentation, wouldn't you agree? So, breathe slowly, take pauses, keep track of those things and a good breathing habit will develop gradually.

Slip sliding away

The structure and delivery of some public speeches often remind me of a tree. Think about it: a speaker, who's visibly distracted, makes a slight diversion from his initial topic, which is point (A), and inserts an interesting story, which takes him to point (B). When he then tries to go back to point (A), he remembers something else he wanted to mention and begins to explain it, which inevitably leads him to point (C), and then (D) and (E) and (F) – as a result, in seconds, he branches off from point (A), creating a beautiful, big "tree", but one that nobody can remember the name of or the reason behind. These kinds of speeches are exceptionally hard to absorb and to stay focused on. They emotionally drain the audience and, when a speaker routinely indulges in these detours to show off his intellect and knowledge of facts, it can quickly become torturous. Keep in mind also that the intellectual level of the audience is always lower than that of each separate individual that makes it up. This is why a "tree-shaped" speech is a sure-fire way to keep your audiences puzzled and confused about what you're saying, even after you have left the stage. During my trainings, I put a picture of such a tree up on the wall as a reminder of what I should not be doing – try adding a tree picture to the notes you take with you to the stage to remember not to slip away from the main point.

Other speeches are like steam trains. The first words set the tone of a very clear and confident speech. And, with them, the speaker begins to move down the rails of his thought, without moving even an inch off the tracks. He goes from the greeting of the audience to the adieus in a similar way that a steam train would go from Newcastle to London – determined and predictable. He makes no stops along the way, no pauses of any kind, leaving his audience inactive and uninvolved in his speech. The speech then becomes primitive and predictable; so predictable, in fact, that the element of surprise evaporates and boredom prevails. Primitivism does not work and things go wrong.

At this point, the reader can ask me, "Well, what do you suggest?" I would first remind you of how a mountain climber gets to the summit – he puts a piton into the mountain, feeds the rope through, pulls himself up, and then screws in the next piton and keeps going. In this way, if he ever falls, he doesn't fall all the way to the bottom of the mountain – just the four or five feet down to the next piton, from where he's soon able to continue his climb. In other words, he is carefully and slowly building on what he has already achieved to avoid killing himself and destroying everything he has done so far. If a mountain climber had to become a public speaker, the structure of his speech would resemble a staircase – where he would try to make every consecutive piece of information he gives memorable to the audience. To do this skilfully and leave a distinctive impression with your listeners, you need to engage with them and pause every step of the way: ask them if everything you're saying is understood; change your location on stage; flip the image on the flip-chart; change a slide; recap the main ideas of what's been said. After you have reached the end of a certain part in your performance, suggest that they ask you questions – this way, you will break up a lengthy speech into shorter, easier to remember and more comprehensive parts, which will be retained much better by the audience. And the best part is, if you make a mistake, it will be forgotten in a second, if it's even noticed at all, because of the very vivid memory of the great parts that came before it. Try drawing a tree, a steam train and stairs – which one of these pictures remind you of your own speeches? Which picture reminds you of a speech you recently heard? Try to analyse this in terms of these three images the next time you listen to a public speaker, and take notes for your own presentations.

How to build success as a public speaker

A German pharmaceutical firm once asked for bids for a contract to provide a series of training sessions for its Russian employees. These sessions were to be on the art of public presentation, and were due to be held in a hotel on the outskirts of Moscow. Needless to say, I was very interested in winning this bid. Seven trainers in total participated in the bid, and the final round was a meeting with the head of the local branch – Nicolas Shultz (his name has been changed to protect his privacy). He was German but spoke very decent Russian. When he entered the conference room, I was prepared to talk to him for an hour or so, explaining in great detail why I thought I was the best person for the job, but after a generic greeting, he said:

"I will not keep you for too long. I only have one question for you: what does one need to do to be a successful public speaker?"

I sneered and said something along the lines of, "Well, you cannot answer this kind of question simply. Two to three days training may not be enough to cover everything. It is a complex phenomenon..."

"Thank you," he interrupted, "we are grateful for your participation in the bid. Good luck!"

"What does that mean?" I asked a friendly staff member, Julia, who was seeing me out of the office.

"You lost the bid," she said with a sigh. "Shultz has had the same reaction to all of you. He heard somewhere that if a person cannot describe what he does for a living in one phrase, he has no idea what he is doing. I too wish you luck!"

I left the beautiful office building and walked towards the parking lot. Straightaway, I was amazed at the stupidity of the situation, and was at first very tempted to blame Shultz for it. But my professional pride was being attacked. What if Shultz was right? That it turns out I don't know anything about public speaking! So what right do I have to teach it?! And so on. This served me well though because, for several days after this meeting, I couldn't stop thinking about it until, finally (maybe because something clicked in my head, or a long-forgotten idea finally shaped itself into a sentence), I found the answer to Shultz's question. And this one answer covered it all – everything my work is about. Everything I knew and everything you are reading about in this book was in one sentence. I called Julia the next morning and asked her to arrange another meeting for me with Schultz.

"Oh, I am so glad you called," she said. "Schultz turned down all the candidates after asking them the same question and we don't know what to do – there's definitely no time to start another bid."

Shultz agreed to meet me and, after we had exchanged pleasantries, I said to him that I wouldn't take up much of his time because the only thing I wanted to say is this:

"The secret of success in public speaking is to talk to people, rather than perform in front of them!"

"Thank you," said Shultz. "We are grateful for your participation in the bid. Good luck!" And he left the room.

"What does this mean?" I asked Julia, confused.

"You won the bid," she said.

Why am I telling you this story? Because this phrase sums up everything I am writing about in this book, in one sentence. When you are on stage, ask yourself this question: am I *talking to* these people or am I *performing for* them?

Can a speaker's mistakes be forgiven?

In the 80s, a small, electronic device called a "drum machine" gained wide popularity in pop music. Musicians no longer needed to transport a whole drum set along with a drummer, because they could just use the "drum machine". It was very convenient for them because, unlike a real rock and roll drummer, it didn't get drunk, didn't get into fights or any kind of trouble, and didn't have creativity crises live on stage. The sound it made was clear and couldn't be distinguished from that of a real drum. And it was crucial for studio recordings. But most real music fans didn't like the device then and still don't like it now. When the company's salespeople did some research into why they weren't that popular, the answer they received again and again was "It's too flawless." So what do you think the clever Japanese manufacturers did? They introduced tiny flaws into the workings of the machine.

So when people ask me how a speaker can achieve pure perfection, I always say that a speaker shouldn't strive to achieve pure perfection; he shouldn't try to become an electronic box without any flaws. Flaws make you human, flaws make you shine, flaws make you unique and beautiful. So don't be afraid of making mistakes, don't be afraid of changing. Changing and growing your skills is in itself a kind of perfection.

FAQ Chapter Ten

1

Dear Radislav, would it be appropriate at meetings or big conferences to use famous advertising catchphrases? Or is it better to quote the classics, because an ad quote might look unoriginal and flat? Let me know please, Vladimir.

Quoting classical literature at mass gatherings? No, please don't. Only mottos and catchphrases; something so popular and contemporary that everyone there will know. Your audience should instantly recognise everything you say at big conferences. Which is why *"Just do it"* or *"Because you're worth it"* would be much more appropriate than *"I have of late, whereof I know not, lost the better part of my mirth..."* But if you are at a meeting of academics and linguists, this is a perfect place for the classics. As so often is the case, it's all about the context – and picking the right catchphrase for your specific audience.

2

Dear Radislav, I perform a lot and often (every day in front of 100 or more people) and get really tired of this. By the end of the day I am exhausted from performing for hours on end, but find it hard to unwind. Can you recommend an easy way to relax Regards, Evgenia.

Evgenia, the easiest way to relax would be to knock back a shot. But with the high-paced work life that you're leading, I wouldn't recommend it, because it could lead to alcoholism, motivation and memory loss, and all kinds of bad outcomes. I must admit, when I started out my career, I was faced with the same difficulties. After my first three-day training session, for example, I was in bed for almost twenty-four hours, not able to get up. I simply could not find the energy – I must have used up all my resources and, at that time, didn't know how to regain them. Even alcohol was not a pleasant option. But, with experience, I learned to distribute my energy in ways that did not leave me drained, and engaged in an energy exchange with the audience, which was very important. Nowadays, I don't feel like I need a lie down at all. For instance, I am writing this email to you in an aeroplane on my way back from Uzbekistan, where I have just conducted two three-day trainings in a row. I got to the airport straight after the sessions and I feel great; I will be working for all four hours of the flight and, when I get home, I will continue to attend to urgent emails and calls. All that happens because I leave the training room with as much energy as I had going in. I cannot explain why this happens. But it's a fact. A lot of speakers, musicians and other public people say that they have the same thing. It is possible that you sometimes also feel an energy rush during your performance and after it. Try to understand what causes it and then you will be able to control the process. As you probably have noticed in life, if someone tells you something negative, your energy levels drop, whereas, after a good compliment, you feel a rush. Give the listeners a chance to tell you to how great your presentation was, whether with applause or a discussion on the topic afterwards. This is good for your group and for you. If you don't have this skill just yet and performances drain you of all your energy, try doing 20 minutes of physical exercise to get your metabolism going and re-energise your body. All the unnecessary elements will leave your skin through sweat and you will feel much better. A sauna can be good for this as well.

3

Dear Radislav, I'm a doctor and I have never been taught anything that resembled psychology or the art of public speaking. Believe me, this is something I know very little about. It's particularly difficult when I need to speak in front of a very diverse group of people with quite a basic knowledge of medicine. I am forced to explain highly complicated things (like syndromes, cures, etc.) in very simplistic terms. How do I do this without descending to a very primitive level of speaking, but at the same time, without my speech becoming boring and overloaded with scientific terms? Would love to hear what you think, Alexey.

A propaganda campaign took place in the USA during the Second World War. Doctors conducted meetings with young mothers, convincing them to give their children fish oil, which is rich in vitamin D, and would keep children safe from rickets. Statistics showed that only 5% of American mothers took this advice, and so the campaign was not deemed successful, even though only doctors with oratorical skills were taking part in it. So the organisers then decided to go a different way and instead, they began asking young mothers to talk about this as well. Women started giving these lectures all over the country. As a result, the percentage of those using fish oil increased to 90%.

The problem is not in the given information but in its source, and if the source is trusted, so will the information be. Put yourself in the place of the people you are performing in front of, and try to talk to them as just a person and not as a doctor. Of course, you can't get completely away from using medical definitions and terms, but try to explain those terms and definitions by relating to your audience. Say things like "pneumonia, or, as we all know it, lung disease", or "vitamin C", instead of "ascorbic acid".

It will be much easier if, instead of speaking about abstract things, you make up a story about a person. But this has to be a person with a biography, name and last name, a job and a location. If the story turns out to be fun and didactic, this speech will become interesting, not only to your patients, but also to your academic colleagues. I wish you luck and health to all your patients!

4

Dear Radislav, as an experienced speaker, you must enjoy your performances very much. But why is it? Is it because in that moment you have power over minds, or because you know you're doing your job well? What exactly is there to love about presentations? I suppose different people find different joys in this, but I am interested in your opinion specifically. What brings you joy in presenting? Elvira.

Your question really made me think for a while. In order to answer it, I looked for parallels. For instance, what would be your favourite moment in eating a beautiful cherry? Is it the smooth, glossy surface or the elastic flesh that easily flakes when you bite into it? Or is it the burst of refreshing juice? Or maybe the slight tickle of the throat, caused by its sweetness? Which of these pleasures do we find most satisfying and which one makes us the most happy?

What do I enjoy during my public performances? The feeling of obtaining power is beautiful, of course; the energy that nourishes the people who have come to an event and shared their time with me is precious too. Essentially, it's a job that has to be done well, because power over minds isn't worth anything if the goal hasn't been reached. Manipulating the audience's emotions in vain is not my thing.

The anticipation before going on stage that's both sour and sweet? The wondering about what the faces are going to be like when they see you? Strained and alert? Or friendly and cheerful? It's the drive of the unknown that brings me there. There are never two performances that are alike, which leaves me wondering how will this time turn out? An obedient and controllable body that helps me deliver my thoughts and feelings to the audience. The pleasure from hearing my own voice come out of the speakers. And even the pleasure of the feeling of loneliness and emptiness afterwards. It is sort of like the feeling when guests leave after a really fun party. The feeling stays with you until the morning. And even that feels awesome. Which one should I chose? What should one concentrate on? I don't know!

I should probably just admit that I can't really answer this question.

At the end of every speech I give, I say this to my audience: "I sincerely wish that you enjoy your public performances! Because anything that is done with pleasure is done right."

About the Author

Radislav Gandapas is one of the most popular Russian coaches in leadership skills. He is a widely-respected authority in the area of communications, public speaking and personal productivity. Radislav is the author of numerous original training sessions, seminars, video courses on oratorical skills, business psychology, and image techniques.

Radislav holds as many as 100 seminars yearly in Russia and the former USSR states, Asia and the Baltics. He has been voted the best in his field by his peers on three separate occasions.

His book, "*A Leader's Charisma*", won the Runet "Book of the Year" award in 2013.

Radislav is a recurring guest expert on numerous TV shows and guest writer in business magazines.

His client list includes some of the biggest companies and banks in Russia, as well as the Sochi Olympic Committee.

For more details go to www.radislavgandapas.uk

Acknowledgements

This book was first published in Russian and quickly became the bestselling book on public speaking in Russia. It has since been translated into Bulgarian and Latvian, and now into English. Many of my colleagues and friends have supported me on the journey of publishing this book in English and have, each in their own way, helped me to make it better for you to read. I would like to take this opportunity to thank them:

Yury Moscaltsov, who helped me take the first steps towards publishing this book in Great Britain, and has since supported me in every way.

Asija Mudrov-Vesty and Dan Vesty, who took upon themselves the difficult task of translating and editing the text before you in its English version.

Vitaly Speransky, who created three different options for the cover that were so nice, I still don't know if I've made the right decision.

Benjamin Araud, whose recommendations and advice have helped me tremendously, and (I hope) will continue to do so for years to come.

Allan Pease, who showed me that such a serious topic can be approached with humour, and who kindly agreed to read the manuscript and give it a preface that I am forever in his debt for.

Ron Hoff, who many years ago, with his book "*I Can See You Naked*" awakened my interest in this topic and pushed me to become an orator.

Bryan Tracy, who has been one of the best examples of a brilliant public speaker out there for many years, and with whom I once had the pleasure and privilege of working.

Anthony Robbins, who constantly pushes back the boundaries of the possibilities for a public speaker.

Richard Denny, who believed in my book and predicted its success.

I would like to also thank each and every one of the tens of thousands of participants in my training sessions all over the world for giving me the material and the inspiration to write this book!

ALSO AVAILABLE

101
TIPS FOR
PUBLIC
SPEAKING

RADISLAV GANDAPAS

For more details go to
www.radislavgandapas.uk

Made in the USA
San Bernardino, CA
14 March 2019